The Rediscovery of
Ethnicity

EDITED BY SALLIE TESELLE

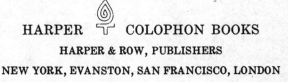

HARPER COLOPHON BOOKS

HARPER & ROW, PUBLISHERS

NEW YORK, EVANSTON, SAN FRANCISCO, LONDON

This work was originally published in the Spring 1973 issue of *Soundings*.

First HARPER COLOPHON edition published 1974

LIBRARY OF CONGRESS CATALOG CARD NUMBER: 73–21152

STANDARD BOOK NUMBER: 06–090367–8

CONTENTS

THE REDISCOVERY OF ETHNICITY:
Its Implications for Culture and
Politics in America

HOW AMERICAN ARE YOU IF YOUR GRANDPARENTS CAME FROM SERBIA IN 1888?

MICHAEL NOVAK

I

NOW THAT THE THEME of "ethnicity" has blazed up again before public eyes, a number of important questions have been raised, a number of objections voiced. What is the meaning of ethnicity? What is the difference between the "old ethnicity" and the "new ethnicity"? Is *everybody* ethnic? What political implications follow?

One of the most interesting developments is the abrupt rejection of ethnic analysis altogether. This rejection is of three types. Those who have been trying all their lives to *get over* their ethnic origin and join the influential mainstream sometimes see the experience of ethnicity as regressive; sometimes don't even want the subject brought up, have vivid emotional reactions against it; sometimes experience a new sense of relaxation and liberation, in a kind of expanded and (at last) integrated self-consciousness.

A second type of rejection occurs among some who have for a time been living in "superculture," that is, in the influential mainstream of power, wealth, and ideas, apart from any ethnic

Mr. Novak is the author of *The Rise of the Unmeltable Ethnics* (Macmillan, 1971), which, he says, he was "trapped" into writing in his attempt to come to terms with himself. His other books—*Belief and Unbelief, The Experience of Nothingness, Ascent of the Mountain Flight of the Dove*—led up to the ethnicity book. He teaches philosophy and religious studies at the State University of New York at Old Westbury. A portion of this essay will appear in *Pieces of a Dream*, ed. Michael Wenk (Center for Migration Studies, 1973).

1

"sub-culture." In the 1930's many intellectuals retained not only an ideological but also an experiential contact with lower-middle-class workers. Since the Second World War the population of superculture has expanded enormously, and now there are millions of educated suburban Americans who maintain almost no contact, ideological or experiential, with ordinary people who work for a living, in blue-collar or white-collar jobs. One sees this gap between cultures on university campuses between faculty and other staff members, or at newspaper offices between the city room and the press room.

It used to be that democracy meant faith in "the common man." But for some time now the common man has come to be perceived as the nation's greatest menace, a racist, a fascist, and—if one is pressed—a pig. All hope is placed in "a constituency of conscience," as opposed presumably to people without conscience. Needless to say, anyone who writes *in support of* the white ethnic is looked upon with puzzlement. What's a nice man like you doing with people like those? . . . This puzzlement sometimes changes to shock, horror, and indignation if the subject is seriously pursued.

Thus passionate intensity is frequently stirred by the theme of ethnicity, most remarkably among people who believe in the universality of reason or love and simultaneously bewail the blandness and mindless conformity of the suburbs. Perhaps this is because the theme of ethnicity intimately involves each participant. Each is challenged to examine his or her own life for its ethnic materials. Almost by definition, these are more unconscious than not, having been taught informally rather than in explicit words or deeds. Gratitude for being prompted to live the examined life is sometimes keen, but sometimes absent.

This invitation to self-examination, moreover, is not simply a use of the *ad hominem* argument. In a reasonably homogenous culture, as in England or France, the terms of discourse are reasonably fixed. In a heterogeneous one like ours, the key terms themselves derive from our different historical experiences of America. Words like "moral" used in politics mean something different to a house mother in a dormitory in a small Ohio college, to Philip Roth, to John Courtney Murray, to Shirley MacLaine, to George Meany, to Jesse Jackson. When you see each speaker in his or her own historical context, the

words make considerably more sense, even if one continues
to disagree. The more sensitive to historical nuance one
becomes, the more intelligible various classical arguments—between sectarian and mainline Protestants, for example—become.
In the United States, our personal histories retain an influential
ethnic and regional component, to which far too little note
is methodologically paid. Thus many of our arguments result
not in mutual understanding but in frustration and separation.

A third type of rejection occurs among some who are quite
unconscious of any ethnicity on their part at all, either because
they're simply white Anglo-Saxons who "don't make anything
of it" or because they're "veritable living melting pots," nobody
having traced the family's intermarriages for years. Anglo-
Saxons who learn English in school, read English literature,
have long learned about the superiority of English political
institutions, and unconsciously accept Anglo-Saxon rituals and
traditions as normative (Thanksgiving dinner without *spaghetti*
or *kolache*, for example) are not aware of being ethnic, because
the mainstream supports their self-image. Only gradually is
the perception dawning that, much as this nation owes the
Anglo-Saxon heritage, it is *not* an Anglo-Saxon nation. It is
a pluralistic nation. What do you do if your grandmother came
to America from Serbia in 1888? The nation is by that increment
also made to be Serbian. But when will the cultural impact
finally be felt? So many things taken for granted by many in
America are unconsciously but effectively ethnocentric. Even
the "civil religion" is defined as Anglo-Saxon Protestant—not
really even German or Scandinavian Protestant.

Values once highly developed in Anglo-Saxon culture, like
those in other groups, are constantly under threat from superculture and its technology—not least that Anglo-Saxon quality
par excellence, civility. University students were just yesterday
attacking even highly civilized parents as "uptight," "effete,"
or "subservient." Shouting, for a time at least, was the moralists'
vogue. The power of television, the cinema, and high mobility
threaten every ethnic culture—which is to say, culture itself.
Values and tastes are taught in families and families need, as
well, public social supports. We have not yet counted the costs
—in anomie, rage, and mindlessness—of allowing families,
neighborhoods, and local cultures to bow to commercial
forces.

As for those who claim to be "veritable melting pots," one usually finds that the more they talk about their families, the more the "significant others" in their family history come into focus. Certain sympathies, certain ways of looking at things, certain mannerisms of thought or behavior are found to have social antecedents. There is a widespread illusion in America that each individual is alone, entirely invents herself, or wholly creates his own style. Our proverbial historical blindness masks from us the ways in which the experience of past generations continues to live on in each of us, passed on in countless tacit ways in the earliest years of our rearing. The generations are amazingly repetitive in their unpredictable cycles.

In a nation as large and diverse as ours, accurate ethnic perception is crucial for mutual understanding. Regionally, in social class, in race, in religion and in ethnic culture, we differ from one another. We use the same words but in the context of different historical experiences. Yet we, of all peoples, have been afraid of ethnicity! We have treated ethnicity as a dirty secret about which we should not speak, except softly, in hopes it would go away. Even our usage of the term "ethnic" reflects our emotional and intellectual confusion. The following dictionary sample, especially in usages 3 and 4, suggests amusing biases:

> Ethnic, adj. 1. *pertaining to or characteristic of a people, esp. to a speech or cultural group. 2. referring to the origin, classification, characteristics, etc. of such groups. 3. pertaining to non-Christians. 4. belonging to or deriving from the cultural, racial, religious or linguistic traditions of a people or a country, esp. a primitive one:* ethnic dances *(The Random House Dictionary).*

"Non-Christian" and "primitive"—these are the images in the background. Not so subtly, "ethnic" is being contrasted with "civilized," from a Western perspective, indeed, from an English perspective.

For good reasons, educated Americans have for a long time hoped that ethnic differences would weaken and disappear. Ethnic conflicts in Europe seem to antedate even the rise of nationalism. Sometimes for generations, nevertheless, ethnic differences seemed not to lead to conflict and a high degree of cosmopolitan interchange was reached. When religious division and nationalism were added to the mix, however, conflicts were brutal and fierce. So it must not be thought that ethnicity is a neutral, unambiguous, or safe part of human consciousness. No part is.

II

What is ethnicity? For some years a loose sense of "ethnic" has been current, as in "ethnic foods." In New York one could easily conjure up images and smells of Jewish, Italian, Chinese, Greek, Black, and other specialties. Would one include turkey, pumpkin pie, plum pudding or fish 'n' chips as ethnic foods? In the United States, "ethnic" was frequently used as a residual category: those who are *not* white, Anglo-Saxon, Protestant. For example, in describing the Tercentenary Celebration of Yankee City, W. Lloyd Warner writes in *The Family of God*, in a chapter entitled "The Protestants Legitimate Their Past":

> those responsible for the success of the Yankee City Tercentenary were conscious of the need for obtaining the wholehearted collaboration of the organizations and churches of ethnic and religious groups. Since almost half the community was of ethnic origin and consciously particpated in groups which identified their members with minority subsystems, and since it was hoped to induce the whole community to participate, the leaders of the celebration, recognizing their problem, were anxious to do everything possible to obtain full cooperation from the various cultural and religious minorities.
>
> Since these groups, including Jews, Poles, Greeks, French Canadians, and others, were all of comparatively recent origin, none being older than about the fourth decade of the nineteenth century, when the Catholic Irish first appeared, to select appropriate symbols for sponsoring ethnic groups and to make assignment of them was a difficult problem for the central committee. Since the interest and main emphasis of those responsible for the subjects chosen was upon periods before the arrival of the new immigrant groups, the problem was even more thorny. The conception of the celebration and the pageant had to do with the Puritan ancestors and the flowering of New England culture; the themes of the great ethnic migrations and their assimilation—the melting pot, the Promised Land, and the goddess of Liberty welcoming them—democracy for all and every kind of race and creed—such themes were nowhere present. Indeed, those who conceived and presented the pageant saw themselves as teachers initiating the new peoples into the true significance of the nation.[1]

"Ethnic," then, is a residual category; it is not used of British-Americans, only of "the others." But ordinary usage went further, even, than that. In America, ethnicity was often viewed as dysfunctional and rather rapidly disappearing. For most groups, "ethnic" meant in effect "meltable." Again, W. Lloyd

Warner, writing this time in *American Life*, may be our witness. He describes a Norwegian Lutheran group in a midwestern city, in which the first and second generations of American-born children, as they grow up, are moved by "the desire to lose the stigma of foreignness." They give up ethnic symbols, including the use of Norwegian. The only remaining formal bond of the group remains the moral bonds structured by the church, its services now in English. "The pressure for Americanization comes only from those who have risen in the class structure of Jonesville. Those who remain in the lower class cling to the traditional behavior of the ethnic group . . . " Perhaps because his attention was drawn to the successful classes, or perhaps because his time-frame was quite long (the word he uses is "ultimately"), Warner continues:

> The number, size, and importance of ethnic groups and sects in American life decrease almost yearly. Many of them are disappearing, and others yield much of their cultural substance to the influences of the outer American world. All increasingly adjust to the major outlines of American society. There are too many factors involved, including those in the ethnic group, America generally, and the larger world society, to predict accurately whether all these groups will continue to exist or will surrender to the forces of assimilation and acculturation, but it seems likely that most, if not all of them, will ultimately disappear from American life.[2]

This seems to be why, in the last decade, the word "ethnic" came to be used not so much for white ethnic groups from Europe, which were presumed to be rapidly "melting," but as a synonym for "minorities," especially those of color: the Blacks, the Latinos, the Indians; i.e., those who visibly were *not* melting. White ethnics were seldom *taught* that they were ethnic. Courses of study about immigrant history—even monographs, or archives, or library collections—were not common; it is amazing how little is known even today. Indeed, strong emotions *against* ethnic identification had been inculcated. For the arrival of over thirty million Catholics and Jews from southern and eastern Europe, as Robert Bellah writes,

> profoundly challenged the American national community. At that point a new conception of community based on cultural pluralism might have developed, and indeed some Americans proposed such a solution. But the main line was quite different. The demand for assimilation, the end of hyphenated Americans, 100 per cent Americanization, all summed up in the image of the melting pot. This image took on graphic form in an event described by Robert Michaelson. For a festival sponsored by Henry

Ford during the early 1920s a giant pot was built outside the gates of his factory. Into this pot danced groups of gaily dressed immigrants dancing and singing their native songs. From the other side of the pot emerged a single stream of Americans dressed alike in the contemporary standard dress and singing the national anthem. As the tarantellas and the polkas at last faded away only the rising strains of the national anthem could be heard as all the immigrants finally emerged. The enormous pressures which created this vast transformation amounted almost to a forced conversion.[3]

Americanization, in short, was a process of vast psychic repression. Anyone with vivid imagination might recreate for himself some feeling for what happened. But even those who in the course of two or three short generations have experienced it have often blocked out its effects from their minds. Again that sensitive Yankee Lloyd Warner describes it objectively:

> The language factor represents a fundamental break between the parent and child, which continually widens as the child grows older. As the schools increase their training of the maturing child in American symbols, his identifications are increasingly with those symbols until more often than not he develops *an active antagonism* to those of his family's origin. . . .
>
> In school not only does the child learn English and the content of American social symbols, but he learns social attitudes that are *opposed* to his family's and his ethnic group's traditional ways of life. . . . In Yankee City it was discovered that ethnic children very often *do not want to play with* children of their own ethnic group but prefer those of other ethnic groups and native Yankees—an indication of their subordination of *the ethnic elements in their personalities* and *unwillingness* to be identified with their own group. . . .
>
> The forces which the dominant society exerts upon the ethnic groups are exerted *primarily upon the child*, so that he, rather than the parent, becomes the transmitting agent of social change. . . .
>
> Although families traditionally have been the central link between the past and the future, *thereby assuring cultural continuity and social stability*, in the ethnic families the culture that is to be transmitted to the children is *rejected* by them; and the changes that are introduced into that cultural system are resisted by the parents and transmitted through the medium of the children. The result is *disruptive to the family system, to the ethnic group, and to many personalities* that experience it.[4]

The cruelty implicit in this process is intense; on first reading, however, one merely accepts it as normal: the inferior learning from the superior. The psychic destructiveness is overlooked. Still, white Europeans—even if a little dark-skinner or otherwise identifiable ethnically—can "pass" in America. It is much more difficult for those whose racial features are more marked. That, perhaps, was the chief reason why the word "ethnic" for a time became increasingly fixed on the minorities of color. A museum of ethnic history, or a chapter in a sociology book, or a listing in a catalog under "ethnic," I found in my researches, was far more likely to lead me to information on Indians, Latinos, or Blacks than on Norwegians, Poles, the Irish, or Greeks.

But there was also another reason. The bias of American intellectual life (and ordinary life as well) is to slight the past, the community, and the imagination, in favor of the future, the individual, and the intelligence. There is a pronounced tendency to underestimate the power of the former and to overestimate that of the latter. Secondly, members of the intellectual community are brought not only into a reasonably affluent social class, but into a class with a significant self-interest in social change. The educated retain relatively little contact, social or intellectual, with lower-middle-class values, aspirations, fears, or insecurities. It is, as Warner suggested, *lower-class* ethnics who remain ethnic longest. The educated undergo far heavier pressures—opportunities?—to "Americanize" than do those who do not go to college, did not (perhaps) go to high school, and do not share in the mythos of college communities. The gap between the educated and the uneducated, indeed, may be more significant—and divisive—in our society than the gap between the rich and the poor.

Hence the intellectual community is liable to neglect a great many important features of American society because of its own sociological position. It has reason, indeed, to be in conflict with other groups in American society: competition for power and status, antagonistic values and modes of behavior, hard questions of freedom and public order. There is a tradition of anti-intellectualism in American life. There is also a correlative tradition of anti-populism: contempt for Main Street, its boosters, and its wavers of flags. We should also add, for completeness, a tradition among our intellectuals of anti-Catholicism—a prejudice with something of an ethnic edge. It is directed not quite so much at English Catholics, who tend to be educated and refined, as at those less graceful and somewhat threatening, heavy-bellied, rather cynical, immigrant working types whose economically progressive politics never quite make up for their way of life.* The photos which editors choose to represent these descendants of immigrants today seem related to the cartoons featured in their pages two or three generations ago.

Since 1967, when the American Jewish Committee held its first national conference on "the white ethnic" at Fordham, the word "ethnic" has been gradually moving back toward its broader usage. Most British-Americans, I believe it will be found, have hardly ever thought of themselves as "ethnic." But that is perhaps true of many Southern and Eastern Europeans, too. The pressure was almost entirely to think of oneself as "American." "We're all Americans!" That is, "We're all equal; I'm just as good as you are." Whatever the sufferings of the past, they are better forgotten. Concentrate on the future.

I have had occasion elsewhere to note that I at first set one condition for the editor of *The Rise of the Unmeltable Ethnics*: that we not use the word "ethnic" in the title. The prejudice, I thought, is so great that many would not read a book with that title; the word gives off bad vibrations—that "stigma of foreignness" Warner wrote of. My favorite uncle handled the new book jacket with gentle wonderment: "We're beyond all that now, aren't we, Michael?" Who wants to remember?

On the other hand, many can't forget. In Newark, in Canarsie, in Forest Hills, in Cicero, in Cleveland Heights, in Warren and in a hundred other places yet unknown to the media there are large concentrations of "white ethnics" who have normally been the vanguard of the only progressive political party we've got, the Democratic Party. In the last few years they have become the fall guy, the villain, in the eyes of many who wish to bring about a greater measure of justice in American society. Richard Daley, George Meany, labor union "bosses," political "machines," cops with little American flags on their uniforms, beer truck drivers, angry crowds . . .

Well, suppose you want to understand what makes people feel the way they do, think as they do—particularly if you notice odd discrepancies in the usual intellectual descriptions of their behavior. For example, construction workers are pictured as

*When you read the word "immigrant," which ethnic groups figure in your imagination? The millions of British-Americans who have arrived here since (say) 1865? Most usage seems to exclude them, as I have here.

pro-war—but according to a Stony Brook study, no profession in New York City in 1970 was more *opposed* to the war than construction workers. Books of political intelligence sometimes call a Slavic district near Pittsburgh "Wallace country"—but Humphrey took 60% of the vote there in 1968, Wallace 14%. 60% is a landslide. Where, actually, did F.D.R., Truman, Kennedy, or Johnson (notably on civil rights) get their majorities? Questions like these raise warning signals about one's own prejudices. What actually is going on among such people? What has their history been like? What in their lives is admirable and beautiful? What are the evils that prey on them? Since all people are evil as well as good, what are their evil tendencies?

Such questions are one part of what is now called "the new ethnicity." For reasons suggested above, the initial focus has been on descendants of immigrants from Southern and Eastern Europe. But if such persons reclaim their own ethnicity, why not others? "Black history" and "Indian history" reopened the study of American history; so did "cold war revisionism." All of a sudden, almost everyone was discovering that the questions "Who am I?" and "Who are we?" led to a much deeper cultural pluralism than we had long been accustomed to imagine. In each of our traditions, good and evil are mixed. Self-discovery does not entail either ethnocentrism or self-glorification. An awakened consciousness of one's social past requires neither chest-thumping nor breast-beating.

During the presidential election of 1972, virtually every national magazine and television news show carried stories on "the ethnic vote." They usually, but not always, meant (as I had in *The Rise of the Unmeltable Ethnics*) "white Catholic ethnic." For they carried a host of *other* stories specifically on the Jewish vote, the Black vote, the Latino vote. In a larger and more accurate sense, of course, all these groups are equally ethnic. Technically and accurately speaking, each of us is ethnic: each human being participates in a particular cultural history (or histories). The fundamental question "Who am I?" includes the question, "Who are we?" This "we" is particular as well as universal, ethnic as well as humanistic. So much is pretty obvious and straightforward.

But practice is not always so obvious and straightforward. Quite commonly, Americans hopelessly misunderstand one another because each fails to note how the contours of his own language and experience differ from those of the other, and neither can find keys to a relevant common culture. We are not skilled in identifying the many senses of reality, styles of exposition, families of symbols, loaded words, and other culturally freighted materials that thrive among us. Some people, of course, observe such cultural cues with great intuitive skill, even without being able to articulate how they do so. The rest of us constantly try—and err. For to catch cues accurately, one must understand both the cultural background and the person. Stereotypes won't suffice.

There are several theses about white ethnics that are conventional but wrong. Let me state them and argue against them.

1. *Ethnic consciousness is regressive.* In every generation, ethnic consciousness is different. The second generation after immigration is not like the first, the third is not like the second. The native language begins to disappear; family and residential patterns alter; prosperity and education create new possibilities. The new ethnicity does not try to hold back the clock. There is no possibility of returning to the stage of our grandparents.

Nevertheless, emotional patterns that have been operative for a thousand years do not, for all that, cease to function. Those of white ethnic background do not usually react to persons, issues, or events like Blacks, or like Jews, or like Unitarians. In a host of different ways, their instincts, judgments, and sense of reality are heirs to cultural experiences that are now largely unconscious. These intuitive leads, these echoes of yet another language, yet another rhythm, yet another vision of reality, are resources which they are able to recover, if they should so choose.

Jimmy Breslin, for example, has lamented the loss of language suffered by the American Irish. He urges Irish Americans to read Brendan Behan: "For a style is there to examine, and here and there you get these wonderful displays of the complete lock the Irish have on the art of using words to make people smile." Breslin loves "the motion and lilt that goes into words when they are written on paper by somebody who is Irish." He compares Behan's tongue to the language of the 100,000 Irishmen marching down Fifth Avenue on March 17: "You can take all of them and stand them on their heads to get some blood into the skull for thinking, and when you put them back on their feet you will not be able to get an original phrase

out of the lot of them. They are Irish and they get the use
of words while they take milk from their mothers, and they
are residing in the word capital of the world and we find that
listed below are the two fine passages representing some of
the most important Irish writing being done in the City of
New York today." He then lists business notices from Brady
the Lawyer and Walsh the Insurance Man.

Jewish writers are strong by virtue of their closeness to the
Jewish experience in America—e.g., their sense of story, and
irony, and dissent. Mike Royko writes with a hard realism and
a blend of humor that is distinctively Slavic; like *Good Solider
Schweik*. Phil Berrigan refers to Liz MacAlister as "Irish," and
shares a traditionally tough Irish priest's suspicion of liberal
intellectuals.

Authenticity requires that one write and act out of one's own
experience, images, subconscious. Such materials are not merely
personal (although they *are* personal) but also social. We did
not choose our grandfathers.

2. *Ethnic consciousness is only for the old; it is not shared by the
young*. It is true that hardly anyone in America encourages
ethnic consciousness. The church, the schools, the government,
the media encourage "Americanization." So it is true that the
young are less "conscious" of their ethnicity. This does not
mean that they do not have it. It does not mean that they
do not feel joy and release upon discovering it. Often, all one
has to do is begin to speak of it and shortly they begin recol-
lecting, begin raising questions, begin exploring—and begin
recovering.

Consider the enormous psychic repression accepted by countless families—the repression required for learning a new language, a new style of life, new values and new emotional patterns, during a scant three or four generations of
Americanization. Many descendants of the immigrants who do
not think of themselves as "ethnic" experience a certain alienation from public discourse in America, from the schools, from
literature, from the media, and even from themselves. Nowhere
do they see representations of their precise feelings about sex,
authority, realism, anger, irony, family, integrity, and the like.
They try to follow traditional American models, of course: the
classic Protestant idealism of George McGovern, for example.
They see a touch of their experience in *Portnoy's Complaint*.

But nowhere at all, perhaps, will they see artistic or political models expressing exactly their state of soul. Nowhere do they find artists or political leaders putting into words what remains hidden in their hearts.

The young are more ripe for the new ethnicity than the old, for the new ethnicity is an attempt to express the experience of *their* generation, not of an earlier generation. It treats past history only as a means of illuminating the present, not as an ideal to which they must return. The new ethnicity is oriented toward the future, not the past.

3. *Ethnic consciousness is illiberal and divisive, and breeds hostility.* The truth is the reverse. What is illiberal is homogenization enforced in the name of liberalism. What is divisive is an enforced and premature unity, especially a unity in which some groups are granted cultural superiority as models for the others. What breeds hostility is the quiet repression of diversity, the refusal to allow others to be culturally different, the enforcement of a single style of Americanism. Our nation suffers from enormous emotional repression. Our failure to legitimate a genuine cultural pluralism is one of the roots of this repression. Our rationalization is fear of disunity; and in the name of unity, uniformity is benignly enforced. (The weapon of enforcement is ordinarily shame and contempt.)

Countless young Italians were given lessons in school on how *not* to talk with their hands; Latin girls were induced to shave their lips and legs; Irish girls to hide their freckles; Poles to feel apologetic about their difficult names; Italians to dread association with criminal activity; Scandinavians and Poles to hate misinterpretations of their taciturnity and impassive facial expression; Catholics to harden themselves against the anti-Catholicism both of intellectual culture and nativist America.

The assumption that ethnic consciousness breeds prejudice and hostility suggests that Americanization frees one from them. The truth is that *every* ethnic culture—including mainstream America, and, yes, even intellectual America—has within it resources of compassion and vision as well as capacities for evil. Homogenized America is built on a foundation of psychic repression; it has not shown itself to be exempt from bitter prejudices and awful hostilities.

America announces itself as a nation of cultural pluralism. Let it become so, openly and with mutual trust.

4. *Ethnic consciousness will disappear*. The world will end, too. The question is how to make the most fruitful, humanistic progress in the meantime. The preservation of ethnicity is a barrier against alienation and anomie, a resource of compassion and creativity and intergroup learning. If it *might* disappear in the future, it has *not* disappeared in the present. And there are reasons to work so that it never does. Who would want to live on a thoroughly homogenized planet?

5. *Intermarriage hopelessly confuses ethnicity*. Intermarriage gives children multiple ethnic models. The transmission of a cultural heritage is not a process clearly understood. But for any child a "significant other" on one side of the family or another may unlock secrets of the psyche as no other does. The rhythm and intensity of emotional patterns in families are various, but significant links to particular cultural traditions almost always occur. One discovers these links best by full contact with ethnic materials. It is amazing how persons who claim themselves to have a "very mixed" ethnic background, and "no particular" ethnic consciousness, exhibit patterns of taste and appreciation that are very ethnic indeed: a delight in the self-restraint of Scotsmen, discomfort with the effusiveness of Sicilians—or, by contrast, a sense of release in encountering Sicilian emotions, a constriction of nervousness faced with the puzzling cues of the culture of the Scots.

Cues for interpreting emotion and meaning are subtly learned, in almost wholly unconscious, informal ways. These cues persist through intermarriage for an indeterminate period. Cues to pain, anger, intimacy and humor are involved. (Many of the passages of *The Rise of the Unmeltable Ethnics* were intended ironically and written in laughter; many reviewers, almost exclusively British-American ones, took them seriously, incredulously.)

6. *Intelligent, sensitive ethnics, proud of their heritage, do not go around thumping their chests in ethnic chauvinism*. Who would want chest-thumping or chauvinism? But be careful of the definition of "good" ethnics, "well-behaved" ethnics. Many successful businessmen, artists, and scholars of white ethnic background carry two sets of scars. On the one hand, they had to break from their families, neighborhoods, perhaps ghettoes, and they became painfully aware of the lack of education and experience among those less fortunate than they. On the other hand, they

had to learn the new styles, new images, new values of the larger culture of "enlightenment." The most talented succeed rather easily; those of lesser rank have quietly repressed many all-too-painful memories of the period of their transition. As surely as their grandparents emigrated from the homeland, each generation has had to carry the emigration farther. Americanization is a process of bittersweet memory, and it lasts longer than a hundred years.

7. *The new ethnicity will divide group against group.* The most remarkable fact about the new ethnic consciousness is that it is cross-cultural. We do not speak only of "Polish" consciousness or "Italian" consciousness, but of "white ethnic" consciousness. The new ethnicity is not particularistic. It stresses the general contours of *all* ethnicity and notes analogies between the cultural history of the many groups. The stress is not only on what differentiates each group but also upon the similarities of *structure* and *process* in which all are involved. In coming to recognize the contours of his or her own unique cultural history, a person is better able to understand and to sympathize with the uniqueness of others'.

8. *Emphasis on white ethnics detracts from the first priority to be given Blacks.* On the contrary, blindness to white ethnics is an almost guaranteed way of boxing Blacks into a hopeless corner. A group lowest on the ladder cannot advance *solely* at the expense of the next group. Any skillful statesman could discern that in an instant. The classic device of the affluent and the privileged is to pretend to a higher morality, while setting the lower classes in conflict with one another.

The most divisive force in America today is, ironically, precisely the "new class" of liberal and radical academics, media personnel, and social service professionals that thinks itself so moral. Perhaps out of guilt feelings—or for whatever reason—they have projected all guilt for "white racism" onto others. And, without undergoing any of the costs themselves, they take sides or plainly appear to take sides in the very sharp competition between lower-class people, white and black, for scarce jobs, scarce housing, scarce openings in colleges, scarce scholarship funds. They take sides not only with Blacks against whites but also with militant Blacks against other Blacks. For almost a decade they have made "white racism" the central motif of social analysis, and have clearly given the impression

that vast resources were going for Blacks, nothing for others.
The "Open Admissions" program in New York City schools,
e.g., was trumpeted as a program for Blacks and Puerto Ricans.
Not much realism would have been required to predict, as
turned out to be the case, that 75% of the students taking
advantage of the program were white ethnics previously unable
to enter colleges.

It is easy for Blacks, at least militant Blacks, to voice their
grievances on television and in the papers. It is extremely difficult to get coverage of white ethnic grievances. They are not
supposed to *have* grievances, it seems, only prejudices. All problems are defined as black-white problems, even when there
are obviously real economic issues for real families in straitened
circumstances. With all good intentions, therefore, the desire
of liberals to give Blacks highest priority has become exclusion-
ary and divisive.

One can still give Blacks highest priority, but in an inclusion-
ary way that aims at coalitions of whites and Blacks on the
grievances they have in common. Newark is divided almost
wholly between Blacks and Italians; Detroit between Poles and
Blacks. Inadequate schools, the dangers of drugs, insufficient
housing, the lack of support for families and neighborhoods
—these grievances afflict white ethnics and Blacks alike. If
these problems are, by definition, problems of race, what sort
of practical coalition can possibly grow? If they are perceived
as problems of *class* (with ethnic variables) there is at least a
practical ground for effective coalition.

In order for a political coalition to work well, people do not
have to love one another; they do not have to share the same
life style or cherish the same values. They have to be realistic
enough to pursue limited goals in line with their own self-
interest. Lower-middle-class Blacks and white ethnics share
more self-interests in common than either group does with
any other. It is on the basis of shared self-interests that lasting
political coalitions are built, and on no other.

9. *Ethnicity is all right for minorities, but not for the mainstream.*
In America, every group is a minority. Even among white Anglo-
Saxon Protestants there are many traditions. What is often
called "mainline Protestantism," centered in the Northeast:
Episcopal, Congregational, Presbyterian, is only one tradition
within a far larger and more complex Protestant reality. The

father of Senator George McGovern experienced prejudice in South Dakota because the kind of Methodist fundamentalism he represented was closer in style to the lower classes, not fashionable either among "mainline" Methodists nor among Germans and Scandinavians, who were mostly Lutheran. Each of these traditions affects the imagination in a different way. British-Americans from small towns in New England live and work in quite different emotional and imaginative worlds from British-Americans who are Brahmins in Boston and New York. Anglo-Saxon Protestants who are dirt-farmers in Georgia, Alabama, or East Tennessee feel just as much prejudice from Northeastern-style settlers as Polish or Italian Catholics: stereotypes of the Southern sheriff and the redneck function like those of the Irish cop and the dumb hard-hat. The Scotch-Irish and the Scots have a vivid ethnic consciousness, as a conversation with John Kenneth Galbraith and Carey McWilliams, Jr., would make plain.

There is no good reason why we do not all drop our pretensions of being *like* everyone else, and attempt instead to enlarge the range of our sympathies, so as to delight in every observed cultural difference and to understand each cultural cue correctly and in its own historical context. Styles of wit and understatement vary. Each culture has its own traditions of emotional repression and expressiveness. Our major politicians are often misunderstood, systematically, by one cultural group or another; the cues they depend on are absent, or mean something else.

III

"The new ethnicity" has at least three components. First, there is a new interest in cultural pluralism in our midst. It calls for a new sensitivity toward others in their differences. It means looking at America alert to nuances of difference, more cautious about generalizations about "Americans." Second, there is the personal, conscious self-appropriation of *one's own* cultural history—a making conscious of what perhaps one before had not even noticed about oneself. This component is a form of "consciousness raising." It is useful because ways of perceiving are usually transmitted informally, without conscious design or articulation. As one makes progress in appropriating one's own complexity, one finds it necessary to give others, too, more attentive regard. Thirdly, there is a willingness to share in the social and political needs and struggles of groups to which one is culturally tied, as a way of bringing about a greater harmony, justice and unity in American (and world) society. Rather than pretend to speak for all, or to understand all, we can each make a contribution toward what we can do best.

Each of these components requires further comment.

(1) Many liberal persons seem to imagine that social progress demands greater unity, and melting away of social differences. The new ethnicity suggests a form of liberalism based on cultural diversity rather than on cultural unity. It argues that diversity is a better model for America, for the self, and indeed for the human race upon this planet. Is the most pressing danger today homogenization or divisiveness? Does the fear of divisiveness breed conformity, fear of difference, repression of genuine feelings? When ethnic cultures and family values are weakened in the pressures of the melting pot, is anything substituted except the bitch goddess success and the pursuit of loneliness? What else might be proposed? How *are* values taught? These questions prompt the new ethnicity.

(2) Some persons are expressly aware of their own ethnic background and interpret the signals from divergent backgrounds successfully. They ask, "What's all this fuss about the new ethnicity?" Well, even their awareness may be first awareness rather than second: accurate enough but not very articulate. It is always a delight to see someone in whom a tradition is alive, even if they *show* better than they *tell*. But in America some of our cultural traditions have been brought to a high degree of articulation and others lie virtually dormant. The Slavs, for example, boast no novel like *Studs Lonigan*, or Mario Puzo's *The Fortunate Pilgrim*, or the whole shelf of American Jewish novels, or even the burgeoning Black literature. How nourishing for the imagination and the sensibility to grow up Jewish, with all that intelligence and energy against which to measure one's own experience, rather than Slavic and virtually solitary. Much remains to be done within many traditions: among Appalachians, Missouri Lutherans, Slovaks, Greeks, etc. And even those which seem to be in stronger shape have strange gaps and self-blindnesses.

(3) The political aims of the new ethnicity are not ethnocentrism, nor group struggle; they are, rather, a greater degree

of justice, equality, opportunity, and unity in American society. But the *strategy* of the new ethnicity is somewhat different from that of, say, George McGovern or the "new politics" generally. From the point of view of conceptualizers of the new ethnicity like Monsignor Geno Baroni, who worked for many years among Blacks in Washington, D.C., the root flaw in the strategy of "the new politics" is that it is unconsciously divisive and self-defeating. It pictures the white ethnic as the enemy. It drives a wedge between the white ethnic and the Black and/or Latino. It fails to extend friendship or insight. It fails to share the daily burdens of the actual struggle for justice in jobs, housing, and schools. *Both* the Black and the white ethnic are defrauded in this society. No doubt the Black suffers more; no one denies that. The question is, how can one most practically *help* him? The response of the new ethnicity is: By helping *both* the lower-middle-class white ethnic *and* the Black together. Otherwise no coalition is possible. Without that coalition, no one advances.

The alternative is that the Republican Party will, as President Nixon has done, reap the benefits of the breakdown of the alliance between the intellectuals and the white ethnics. A drop in the Slavic Democratic vote from 82% to 60% is a catastrophe for Democrats; and it does not have to happen. If the university wing of the Democratic Party sides with the Blacks *against* white ethnics, and sets up a social pattern whereby gains for Blacks are possible only as losses for white ethnics (or vice versa), the outcome is plain—and deplorable. The social pattern must be fair to *all* groups. Divisive tactics are fatal.

It is not necessary to idealize white ethnics in order to construct a social scheme within which it would be to their advantage to work for equality for Blacks in jobs, housing, and good schools. It is not even necessary to *like* white ethnics. But it does help to understand their history in various parts of America, their spiritual resources, and their chronic weaknesses. Fear of the new ethnicity is very like the early fear of "Black power." Even some Blacks sound, with regard to the new ethnicity, like some whites with regard to Black pride. Such fears must be proven groundless.

If we knew all we had to know about Poles, Italians, Greeks, and others in America, there would perhaps be no need for the almost desperate tones with which the new ethnicity is sometimes announced. But the fact is, we know very little about them. Our anthropologists know more about some tribes in New Guinea than about the Poles in Warren or Lackawanna. We have encouraged too few of the talented white ethnics to stay with their people and to give voice to their experience. Local political leadership is often at a very low level. Community organizers who spring from the community are all too few. Uncle Toms are many. If there is anomie, fear, or rage in such communities (often there is a great deal of bottled-up political energy and great good will), it is to no one's advantage.

The new ethnicity gives promise of *doing* something creative in such places. The new ethnicity is the best hope of all who live in our major urban centers. What we have without it is not promising at all.

NOTES

1. W. Lloyd Warner, *The Family of God* (New York, 1961), p. 144.
2. W. Lloyd Warner, *American Life* (Chicago, 1965), pp. 204-205.
3. Robert Bellah, "Evil and the American Ethos," *Sanctions for Evil*, ed. Nevitt Sanford and Craig Comstock (San Francisco, 1971), p. 181.
4. Warner, *American Life*, pp. 188-90 (emphasis added).

TO SEE THE "ME" IN "THEE":

Challenge to ALL White Americans, or, White Ethnicity from a Black Perspective and a Sometimes Response to Michael Novak

AGNES MORELAND JACKSON

Nᴏᴛ ʏᴇᴛ ꜰʀᴇᴇ more than three hundred years after being brought to these shores, and more than one hundred years after the so-called emancipation of slaves, many Blacks in the U.S.A. are wary of—indeed, frightened by—current national emphasis on white ethnicity. *White* people seeking more rights on a land that has established white *as* right? *White* people chiding Blacks for continually exposing this nation's systematic and systemic racism?* *White* people chiding other whites—liberal WASPS and Jews—for responding to the needs of Blacks while allegedly ignoring the needs of other whites? To many Blacks in this country these questions describe an astounding situation. To many Blacks the recent and increasingly loud cries of white ethnic Americans sound like a resurgence of the white backlash against the Civil Rights Act of 1964.

Not now or ever will we understand all the meanings or implications of white ethnicity. But one possible meaning worth

Ms. Jackson is a member of the English faculty at Pitzer College and the Black Studies Center at The Claremont Colleges, Claremont, California. Previously she taught at Boston University and California State University, Los Angeles. She also serves as consultant to school districts initiating courses in literature by Black Americans.

*Some think that civil rights legislation and social movements in support of civil rights make continual watchfulness unnecessary. Many should have noticed, however, that the same racism that had diminished or become more subtle in the South as a result of national concern is now expressed more openly by non-Southern citizens.

examining is that of racism, a suggestion shared with Michael Novak in October, 1971 when I said that white racism by any other name is racism still. After reading his articles and a full-length book,* I maintain that view. Although based more on experience than on scholarly research, this response and the validity it claims can be justified by exploring three topics (or perhaps taking three glances at one persistent reality): the importance of whiteness in our society, the relationship between white ethnics and Blacks in the blue-collar labor market, and some problems relating to the "now" emphasis on white ethnicity. Such a consideration might explain why Blacks in this country direct a challenge to white ethnics and to *all* whites in the U.S.A.

To Be Is To Be White

Informing my intellectual perception on what my experiences and gut feelings long ago taught me to be true—namely, that whites in the U.S.A. project and accept themselves as *white* first, no matter how unique or interesting they are in other dimensions of themselves—is an article by Armando Morales called "The Collective Preconscious and Racism," which makes much use, in turn, of some ideas coming from the early years of sociology. The key idea is that a "collective experience of the race" shapes a person's experience and "makes a man accept what he cannot understand, and obey what he does not believe.

---

*Michael Novak's *The Rise of the Unmeltable Ethnics: Politics and Culture in the Seventies* (New York, 1971). Despite its abundant and helpful information and its apparently valid discussion of white ethnics' experiences in frustration and richness of culture, their aspirations, and possible solutions to the problems that plague our society, this book is poorly organized and expresses toward Blacks attitudes that are puzzling in their contradictions. Most readers of Novak's book will have noticed the qualities that identify it as a patchwork of hostility and admiration (sometimes sympathy) for Blacks. Part of this article considers some examples of unrelated statements and their resultant derogatory implications, uncritical assumptions and generalizations about Blacks as part of the national culture, and contradictory representations of white ethnic attitudes toward Blacks. But because these instances may reflect only Novak's having tried so diligently to shock WASP and Black militant readers that he neglected ordinary concern for clear organization, these criticisms should *not* be construed as an attack on Novak himself. To date, ours is a cordial and respectful relationship that should benefit from his knowing the responses of a Black colleague to his published ideas on culture and our society.

His thoughts are only partly his own; they are also the thoughts of others.... His standard is outside."[1] This "consciousness of kind" has the following effect on *social conduct*: "Within racial lines the consciousness of kind underlies the more definite ethnical and political groupings.... Our conduct towards those whom we feel to be most like ourselves is *instinctively* and rationally different from our conduct towards others, whom we believe to be less like ourselves."[2] The United States of America understands herself to be a *white* nation, and *white* is the basic status or attribute and the basic identity of all white Americans, including white ethnics.

But no observant adult in this country needs sociological reports to tell him or her that the absolute division of people in this country is determined by whether they are white or non-white.* And because Whites control this country, all white people derive, and have derived, from our caste society material benefits and opportunities for development denied to non-whites.† Furthermore, regardless of the numbers or the percentage of Blacks who share in the material comforts of the U.S.A., and notwithstanding the also special history of the native Americans (the Indians), Blacks in our society symbolize all other non-whites because Blacks represent to whites *the extremity of otherness*. It is this realization that forces the conclusion among Blacks that racism is and has been the primary cancer in the bowels of America. Historically and traditionally, the exclusion and the segregation of Blacks defined *color*—real or imputed, as in the case of people who look "white" but are known to have blood relationships with Blacks—as the basis of dividing our society into two camps. It matters not, therefore, what the

---

*Novak's statement in *The Rise of the Unmeltable Ethnics*, p. 8, is correct: "The white-black polarization is gross. There are many cultural streams among both blacks and whites." However, Novak seems not to appreciate fully how the "*cultural* streams" have been polluted by the *racial* dichotomy.

†"Caste" in this discussion means *racial* distinctions and divisions in the U.S.A. between white people and all non-white people (collectively as non-whites or in their distinct groups: various Asians, Indians, the Spanish Caucasian and Indian mixed blooded people, primarily from Mexico, called Chicanos, and African Americans, here called Blacks). These groupings are non-voluntary in that people belong by virtue of their existence. Were racism to be overcome, however, the distribution of wealth, power, and opportunities available to any members of the total society would not be determined by, or related to, *caste*.

varieties of class and ethnic divisions are among Whites.* The governmentally established and popularly sanctioned *basic* division between people in this country is racial: whites on one side and Blacks and all other non-whites on the other. Had this basic division not been understood, the civil rights movement that dates from the early Sixties would have had an entirely different character. Of course, many of the leaders and followers of that movement must have realized that, by helping to free Blacks, they would be advancing the freedom of all who were denied for reasons of caste and class. But the primary concern of that activity was to end the nation's legal and social oppression of Blacks.

How absolutely our society recognizes the polarities of white and black is suggested by the language of reformers in areas other than race relations. For example, Jerry Farber's *The Student as Nigger* makes clear by its title the extremity of alleged oppression against students. Charles A. Reich discusses a system of "meritocracy" that makes *any* worker, "white or black, into a 'nigger' who despises himself" and describes the workers of the new generation as people who "will not be servile . . . will not be a 'nigger' while on the job."[3] Perhaps only a few have

---

*In the appropriate context, however, these divisions should not be minimized. Ethnic whites have desired and achieved assimilation into "mainstream" white America while even the Blacks who might have wanted to be absorbed could never be. Sinclair Drake and Horace R. Cayton, in *Black Metropolis: A Study of Negro Life in a Northern City* (1945; reprinted New York, 1962), I, 17-18, observe that

> The entire history of Chicago from its birth to the First World War was characterized by the struggle, sometimes violent, of the first-comers and native-whites against the later immigrants—the "foreigners." In the Sixties it was everybody against the Irish and the Irish against a handful of Negroes and Hungarians; in the Seventies it was the Know-Nothing native-Americans against the Germans, Irish, Scandinavians, Bohemians, Slavs, and Frenchmen; in the Nineties, the northern Europeans and native-whites against the southern and eastern Europeans, the so-called "new immigration."

> However much the native-born and older immigrant groups might dislike the "new immigration," they needed these people in order to maintain their own social and economic hegemony. . . . As the immigrants arrived, the native-born were able to move up in status. . . . Wherever hot, heavy, or dirty work was to be done—here were the latest batches of immigrants, starting in at the bottom, but planning to get ahead themselves, or to push their children ahead. The children, once they had gone through the public schools, might be expected to move out of the slums, get better jobs, and *lose themselves* among the older American groups [Italics added].

noticed the ease of expression by whites stating their refusal to play the "nigger" role, but this linguistic generalization is very significant as a by-product of assumed racial superiority. Among other possibilities, the use of such language by whites exemplifies their self-understanding that they can be anyone and can appropriate any quality or characteristic—even nigger-hood.* The language itself thus confirms that the absolutely lowest status is represented by blackness, as a result of a complex, nightmarish history of exploitation and oppression that makes this society shrink from being black. Nevertheless, while acknowledging the extremity of this country's harshness toward her Black citizens and expressing the revulsion of some whites from the worst conditions of oppression, this use of "nigger" to define the worst condition in any situation is based on the complete alignment in this country of whiteness and high self-esteem.

In fact, so aligned with whiteness is self-esteem that *not to be Black* is a state of blessedness. Precisely because in this country *to be is to be white*, millions of whites have assuaged their pain of poverty, disease, and ignorance with the balm of "At least I ain't a nigger." Because in the U.S.A. *to be is to be white*, millions of non-Nordic European immigrants have learned, used, and thrown in the faces of American Blacks the word "nigger" and other words that make clear the distinction between themselves and Blacks. Not duration in the land, not contributions to the nation, not facility with the English language or smooth practice of social customs, not even the giving of life for the nation—none of these has been so effective as *not being niggers* in the socialization of Caucasian immigrants to this country. So obvious has this been to Blacks in both rural and urban areas that a saying among us is "After they step off the boat, the first word they learn is 'nigger.' " And the

*Consider the wearing of Afro or "natural" wigs by white women. The truth is that no identity is safe from encroachment by whites, and neither is any ethnic style beyond their appropriation—as suggested by Reich's comments (pp. 236-37) on aspects of clothing worn by the new generation to "express" themselves: "a headband can produce an Indian, a black hat a cowboy badman." What Reich expresses most clearly by this example, however, is his own unconscious racism. As for affluent white college youths' wearing "something that sells for $4.99 from coast to coast" (p. 238), to Reich and other liberal whites it might "express profoundly democratic values"; but to really poor students this affectation of poverty is obscene mockery. And how does one define the deliberate tearing and aging of the inexpensive "democratic" clothes?

learning intensified from the first to the third generations. "Those people with the funny names" *have* caught hell from other white Americans; but Blacks of any name have caught hell from *all* whites. That some white racists are "foreign" or the descendants of "foreigners" has complicated rather than eased the bitterness of Blacks, for the most educated and cultured Blacks have experienced exclusion and injustice from immigrant whites (often acting as agents of dominant whites) who speak in broken English and thick accents. Even while recognizing the hurt in the lives of such immigrant whites, and certainly not subscribing to the ideational sickness that values humans according to their facility with the English language, their education and culture, or their style, and understanding clearly the apparently *human* need to have a scapegoat, many Blacks, nevertheless, see the primary "value" being upheld by such immigrants as the value of whiteness, the value of *not being a nigger*.

Not being a nigger gives assurance to the European-accented voice of the manager who says, "We don't rent to Negroes," as I was told in 1957 by the manager of an apartment building owned by the best-known university in New York City.* Not being a nigger even helps the second-generation Japanese American apartment manager stand very tall as he tells me the same thing—this time in Los Angeles in 1964. Whether it's being shunned by swarthy American Caucasians or dark-skinned Pakistanis and East Indians while being sought out by fair Caucasians (who in their fair skins do not risk being identified as nigger—the risk run in this country by Indians and Pakistanis and other dark-skinned peoples), or being stared at (or ignored) as someone out of my "place" by white clerks, secretaries, professors (often my colleagues), and college presidents, all of whom are getting used to black *student* faces but not black *faculty* faces, I know personally—and millions of other Blacks know—that for this country the chief qualifier of worth is a "white" skin.

---

*As a student at the university, I was eligible to sub-lease the apartment for the summer. The elderly white woman to wanted to sub-let seemed pleased that I might be her tenant; the apartment manager was not. University officials tried to evade the issue, but I was finally allowed to move in. I learned many months later that the university had cited my having lived in the apartment as evidence that no racial discrimination had ever been practiced.

Other non-whites also know this, hence their long-standing acquiescence and sometimes participation in the naming of niggers. How else, except by naming the niggers, could the Asians and the Mexicans make their own non-whiteness less a badge of shame in this country that considers whiteness a superior characteristic?* The "how else" might have been answered formerly with words like "self-pride" and "dignity," but only now —as a result of the niggers ourselves establishing our own names and values and exposing the nation's total oppression against Blacks—is our society beginning to understand that cultural pluralism and racial and ethnic pride are indeed the name of the game. Until yesterday, however, our society had duped non-whites as well as white ethnics into believing that we were in the mythical pot of democracy and equality, thus prompting our self-mockery as we sought to be *melted*. For the non-black non-whites the deception was especially cruel, because "At least I ain't a nigger" obscured for them the reality of their own oppression.

I would not blame other non-whites for naming the niggers, just as I cannot blame Blacks for our various roles in attempting to overcome our blackness; for until now almost all of us identified the faces and values of white people as the epitome of worth, the summit, the top rung of a ladder whose several lowest rungs we occupied.† We thought that to progress meant

---

*American Indians are outside this generalization. The traditional scorn for Blacks expressed by some Indians has been based on Blacks' having "submitted to" slavery. Notwithstanding popular knowledge that a traditional attitude among whites is that "the only good Indian is a dead Indian," it seems that to Indians more worth derives from fiercely resisting oppression—even to near-extermination—than from endurance, survival, and development in spite of oppression. Today, however, along with other people of color in the U.S.A., native Americans recognize the leadership of Blacks in the affirmation of human dignity.

†In "What the Melting Pot Didn't Melt," *Christian Century*, 89 (April 19, 1972), 441, Michael Novak talks of white ethnics uniting "with other ethnic groups at the bottom of the social ladder." A more accurate statement would be that while white ethnics do share the *lower* rungs of the social ladder, the racist philosophy and practice of this nation have reserved for Blacks the bottom, the *lowest* rung. A study by Martin T. Katzman, reported in "Urban Racial Minorities and Immigrant Groups: Some Economic Comparisons," *American Journal of Economics and Sociology*, 30 (Jan. 1971), 15-17, seems to support this view. To explain the poorer economic performance of six racially distinctive minorities in contrast to the performance of white immigrants, Katzman suggests that "*subcultural* and *discriminatory* differences

to become as white as possible—at least with regard to values, mores, and styles.* Among us it was the Blacks' role to occupy the lowest rung of the developmental ladder, a depth to which other non-whites might fall but only for the duration of their not being able to prove that they weren't niggers. Another of my personal experiences illustrates this point.

In the late Fifties in New York City, when for two summers I worked in the home missions departments of two major Protestant denominations, I helped to process dossiers of displaced families (and of some children alone) from Indonesia and Hungary. After establishing the host families' abilities to be sponsors and friends, the churches' *major concern* about placing the refugees in the South and in some sections of the Midwest and West was the refugees' darkness of skin. My white supervisors knew that to be mistaken for a nigger in some parts of the U.S.A. would have been the cruelest hurt. Perhaps of paramount concern in this was the image of the nation and that of the Christian churches as havens for those fleeing "the Communists": No more serious damage could have been inflicted on those images than to have had refugees from Communist tyranny experience the total oppression reserved for Black citizens of this land of freedom.

The Dignity of Work

Materials that I know on the subject of white ethnicity emphasize the urban-dwelling, blue-collar work status of most ethnic whites.[4] The building trades, coal mining, steel and automobile manufacture, railroading and the whole transportation industry, road construction, longshoring—these are some of the areas of work that "blue-collar" denotes. With the exception of coal mining, however, in these and other labor markets the Blacks have been and still are discriminated against.[5] Among

may be hypothesized to overwhelm any similarities between the European immigrants and the racial minorities." Moreover, he concludes (p. 24) that Orientals "face less prejudice from the white population than the Negroes."

*Novak is exactly right on this point. On p. 114 of *The Rise of the Unmeltable Ethnics* he says that "all ethnic groups have their own confusions. All acceded for far too long to the pressures of Americanization—which was really WASPification."

unionized laborers the position of Blacks has in general moved merely from exclusion to discrimination.* Currently a new consciousness among Blacks has caused blue-collar workers among us to bring more pressure on industry and business to eliminate racial discrimination.[6] While accepting the statements of white ethnics that they are "the working class" and hold primarily "blue-collar" jobs, and without going into the details of union organization and apprenticeship procedures, as a Black American I must also raise the question of the relationship of white ethnics to labor's discrimination against Blacks.

Competition for jobs seems always to have pushed people into adversary roles,† and racial hatred was fostered by management's deliberate use of Blacks as strike-breakers during the early years of labor's attempts to organize. In addition, whenever whites would take certain jobs—even those regarded as "Negro" jobs—white employers often favored white workers over black workers. That the white workers were frequently European immigrants just complicated the early problems of

---

*Especially interesting on Blacks and labor unions are Franklin's comments in *From Slavery to Freedom*, pp. 400-402. Acknowledging the lack of skills among "most" of the Negroes who might have sought membership in most of the "craft unions," he says that "the urban Negro laborer, both in the North and in the South, was essentially faced with the problems of obtaining membership in the labor unions that came more and more to dominate the industrial picture. Prejudice against the Negro worker and the refusal of numbers of whites to work with Negroes served to exclude many from membership." Although the AFL "at first . . . took a positive stand" against discrimination against Negroes, "the leaders . . . .began to realize that this unequivocal stand on the race question was preventing the expansion of the organization, for some independent craft unions which would not accept Negro memberships refused to join." Consequently, the more powerful unions like the National Machinists' Union were allowed to join the AFL if they "did not openly exclude Negroes. . . ." That is, "the exclusion . . . was merely transferred from the constitution to the ritual, and members were pledged to present for membership only white workers." Franklin concludes (p. 436) that organized labor evinced a "pronounced feeling of hostility. . . . Only the Cigarmakers' International Union and the United Mine Workers of America seemed to welcome Negroes into membership, although some other unions had Negro members."

†In *From Slavery to Freedom* (p. 436) Franklin records, for example, that at the turn of this century when the American city was growing rapidly, "employment opportunities were fewer than the number of people coming to urban areas, and Negroes found great difficulty in securing anything except the more onerous and less attractive jobs."

animosity between Blacks and ethnic whites.* The prominence
of white racism in the ranks of labor today suggests, however,
that many white ethnic Americans participated with other whites
in oppressing Blacks. (The Poles in the United Mine Workers
of America are an interesting exception to this. If the U.M.W.
is "largely Polish," as ethnic white Barbara Mikulski asserts,[7]
then they deserve some credit for that union's history of having
always "freely admitted Negroes to membership, even in the
South."[8])

In raising these few questions about white ethnics, labor, and
Blacks, I am responding in part to the white ethnic writers—especially Michael Novak—who generalize about the "working
class" and the "working man." What is meant, of course, is
that white ethnics constitute a large group among working-class
Americans. What seems to be implied is that white ethnics have
worked hard, while other ethnics seek an easier route to success.[9]
But achieving self-respect and "moderate success" through honest labor honestly rewarded has been an option less available
to Blacks than to white ethnics. Henry Miller's catalogue of
workers—those "steam fitters, iron molders, cops, bartenders,
motormen, pipe-case makers, butchers, bakers, shoemakers and
so on"—did not include many *Black* fathers because they were
excluded from many of those jobs.[10] Among the crafts and
skills that are, according to Novak, "dying of starvation in
America," the specific jobs of "masonry, carpentry, woodwork,
. . . furniture making . . . and tailoring" have also not been

---

*In *Black Metropolis*, I, 233 and 235, Drake and Cayton cite an 1885 report
of a "prominent colored woman [who] was deploring the fact that Negroes
were beginning to lose their monopoly in certain fields: 'It is quite safe to
say that in the last fifteen years, the colored people have lost about every
occupation that was regarded as peculiarly their own. Among the occupations
that seem to be permanently lost are *barbering, bootblacking, janitors in office
buildings, elevator service,* and *calcimining.* White men wanted these places and
were strong enough to displace the unorganized, thoughtless, and easy-going
occupants of them. When the hordes of Greeks, Italians, Swedes, and foreign
folk began to pour into Chicago, the demand for the Negro's places began.
One occupation after another that the colored people thought was theirs
forever, by a sort of divine right, fell into the hands of these foreign invaders.' "

In *From Slavery to Freedom*, p. 400, Franklin writes, "The Southern urban
Negro even found it difficult to render his customary personal services. Bar-
bers met with foreign competition, while cooks and caterers were displaced
by the palatial hotels which frequently did not hire Negroes. Everywhere
there was sentiment against hiring Negroes in jobs that had even the semblance
of respectability."

as available to Black as to white ethnic craftsmen. Still there have been and are Black urban craftsmen, notwithstanding the "largely rural base of skills" exhibited by Blacks (Novak, p. 230).

Among "electricians, truck drivers, and construction crews" (Novak, p. 246) Blacks are disproportionately few, given our abilities in these areas. Another personal illustration is pertinent. When in the 1930's as a postal clerk in the Brooklyn General Post Office my father-in-law (fortunate enough even in the 1920's to have learned an electrician's skills but restricted from earning his family's living by those skills, hence the job in the post office) sought to join the post office's electrical crew, he was not allowed to, despite having been recommended by a white ethnic—Jewish—member of the crew who was reportedly amazed and pleased by the extent of my father-in-law's knowledge of electricity. Why couldn't he join the post office electricians? They wouldn't tolerate a "nigger" working with them. The oral history of my family contains still another instructive illustration. In sharp contrast to being excluded from the jobs in electricity, many Blacks *in the South* drove interstate truck routes before such jobs paid fairly good wages. When the living of truck drivers promised to be relatively "good," however, Blacks were displaced by whites. Black folk history—the only accurate history about some of this nation's past—is also full of references to Black railroad firemen who guided trains across hundreds of nearly desolate southern miles but who had to resume their firemen's roles when the trains approached the towns and cities. Ironically, these Black firemen who could guide trains were to lose even their firemen's jobs when such work became more rewarding economically. Who got the jobs? Whites, including many ethnics whose capacity to "work like dogs" Novak (p. 248) calls "good, human, and dutiful, . . . [a source of] pride."

Blacks who also worked or could work like dogs often learned that not to be white was not only *not to be*, but also not to be retained or hired. To labor or to be willing to labor was frequently not enough if the laborer was black. White ethnics, therefore, need to reexamine their claims to, and their seemingly racist implications about, dignity through work.

The "Now" Of White Ethnicity, Or, White Ethnics,
Blacks, and Finding the Self

There is a time for all things. Now—the Seventies, decade
of the ethnics, says Novak—is the time for white ethnics to
assert themselves toward the goal of finding and fulfilling their
true identity. Because of my opinion—shared by many Blacks
and some whites—that racism is still the lethal cancer of our
society,* I am concerned lest white ethnicity join ecology and
women's and gay liberation in preventing or forestalling our
nation's accepting fully the truths about its racist self that the
civil rights movement and the new Black affirmation have raised
in the national consciousness. Blacks cannot with Novak (p.
19) "suppose that in the 1960s the blacks and the young had
their day in the sun, [that] they had maximum publicity, and
[that] now it is the ethnics' turn [who] perhaps . . . can carry
our society further, more constructively, more inventively."
Blacks cannot share these suppositions because, until *racism*
ceases to be *the* "American" way of life, *every day* will have to
be the Blacks'. In the U.S.A. there could be no more progressive,
constructive, or inventive social development than whites' learning to confirm themselves, their humanity, in black and other
non-white sharers of this nation's pain and possibility. Malcolm
X is wholly correct in saying that it is white people who seem
to be "tone deaf to the total orchestration of humanity."[11] How
ironic it is, therefore, that one trying to understand this new
assertion is aided by knowledge of the new Black consciousness;
for white ethnics surely took their cue from that movement.†
In his phrasing of this opinion, an editor of the Catholic

*I use "white racism" in spite of agreeing with Novak that it is being used
by many for political gain, that is, that "the phrase 'white racism' has become
for the Left what 'communism' was for Joe McCarthy: an indiscriminate
scare word designed to prevent clear thought and apt strategy" (p. 7). In
the present discussion the term is appropriate, even indispensable.

†Although white ethnic Barbara Mikulski says that the "new militancy"
of white ethnics is "not necessarily" derived from the civil rights movement
but is related to the "tradition of direct action in the labor unions" (in Clancy,
"The Ethnic American—An Interview with Barbara Mikulski," p. 559), Novak
supports the point I have made, both in *Unmeltable Ethnics* and in "What
the Melting Pot Didn't Melt," p. 89, where he states that the new Irish pride
in identity is "more properly" attributed to "those who raised the black consciousness," than to the Jews, as a Pete Hamil reportedly asserts.

magazine *America* emphasizes an aspect of white ethnicity that should be examined in the context of questioning its possible racism. Thomas Clancy writes that "Black nationalism caused the white ethnics to remember what they had been taught to forget, their own origins."[12]

White ethnics surely did learn to forget their origins, and in learning that lesson so well they have become full partners with Anglo and Nordic whites—the WASPs—in the racist conspiracy against non-whites, especially Blacks.* In "The Price of Being Americanized"—his opening remarks in *Unmeltable Ethnics*—Novak has not specified the learning of *racial* prejudice among the injuries suffered by his grandparents as they sought to become "full Americans." But he acknowledges such learning among white ethnics generally, citing Mike Royko's description of the immigrant as bringing old prejudices to, and acquiring new prejudices in, the New World: "The ethnic states got along just about as pleasantly as did the nations of Europe. With their tote bags, the immigrants brought all their old prejudices, and immeidately picked up some new ones. An Irishman who came here hating only the Englishmen and Irish Protestants soon hated Poles, Italians, and blacks. A Pole who was free arrived hating only Jews and Russians, but soon learned to hate the Irish, the Italians, and the blacks."[13] It's perfectly clear. No matter what the lines of hatred *among themselves*, the white ethnics could also direct hatred toward Blacks. White racism has always been a "family" affair—the family of whites who, despite their in-group antagonisms, still agree on the subject of niggers.

Therefore, merely to mention the economic and other insecurities of Chicago's ethnic whites who became a hate-filled mob when Martin Luther King, Jr., led marchers for open housing does not consider the basic fact of racism. Novak seems not to have understood the full import of his saying (on pp. 12-13) that the "ethnic Catholics" who have become racists "since their arrival in this nation" are getting "sick to death of being

---

*The white ethnics' complicity in having sought and—so far as their capacity to name the niggers is concerned—having *achieved equal whiteness* with the WASPs is not mitigated by their having been inspired by black consciousness or by their cause being championed by articulate Christian scholars. Moreover, valid claims that might have been made in *any* era seem to be stated *now* in antithesis to, or in order to dilute, the valid claims of Blacks.

moralized" by the "accusing, jabbing finger of Protestant moralists."* Note the emphasis (p. 13) upon the feelings of white ethnics: they "cannot tolerate" anyone's intensifying their "guilt." Instead, they can be won over by "congratulating them for their loyalty as Americans." While Novak may not know the full meaning of what he says, Blacks do. "Loyalty as Americans" has meant, to most whites, acquiescence in, or active support of, this nation's whites' thinking themselves superior to Blacks, whose alleged inferiority is then used to justify any wrong toward us.

Ironically supporting my view that the basic life style of all whites in this country is to "name the niggers," Novak assumes an accusatory tone in most of his comments about white ethnics vis-a-vis Blacks. Although Blacks are praised for having stimulated the self-appreciation of other racial and ethnic groups and for having created the national climate in which those groups might raise their voices, they still are made to share the blame for the nation's slowness to open its ears to the voices of white ethnics. It's not enough that Chicanos and Indians and Asians have blamed Blacks for getting "too much" of the belated and insufficient concern dragged out of this country by black people's voices, black people's efforts, black people's "dues," including physical hurt unto death. Now the white ethnics plead their causes in the context of how much the dominant white group is doing for Blacks or its receptivity to the point of view of Blacks.[14]

For example, Novak states (p. 7) that, in contrast to their responses to "prejudices against blacks," leaders of the political Left "have seldom" challenged "prejudices against ethnic Americans." But what remains unstated is that white ethnics themselves have fostered such indifference by participating with dominant whites in the culture of white superiority. Therefore, as I have said, to chide other whites for their expressed concern for Blacks is to imply that the Blacks are at fault for the neglect of ethnic whites. Novak draws the following analogy on p. 80: "The new immigrants were to the old Americans the double threat that the blacks have become for ethnics today. A pattern of racism and superpatriotism was held over the heads of the

---

*This contradicts the forceful passage on p. 60: "Racists? Our ancestors owned no slaves," and thus illustrates again the poor logic of *Unmeltable Ethnics*.

ethnics." He also develops a full chapter on "The Nordic Jungle: Inferiority in America'" and explains on p. 81 how the swarthy Southern and Eastern European immigrants suffered "white racism" by being "drawn into the orbit of associations linked to 'black.'" However, Novak's observation on the same page that America's "pride in the English heritage gradually became pride in the Anglo-Saxon-Teutonic heritage, and [that] the latter was all too near to pride in the Nordic race," ignores the discrimination against *black* people even in the "English heritage."* The truth uglier than the white ethnics' suffering "Nordic racism in America" (p. 87) is that of the Blacks' suffering *white* racism in America. Blacks in this country feel the weight of the *whole* category called *white*.

Again not seeming to have understood the full significance of his words, Novak shares (p. 65) another truth as ugly and painful: In response to humiliations from "nativist" whites, immigrant parents "began to go out of their way in order to act American." A damning consequence was the immigrants' subversion by racism that taught them to regard their whiteness as their primary virtue.† Even more significant, therefore, than

---

*Ironically (because he does not follow the idea to its ultimate conclusion about white ethnics and racism), Novak provides evidence (from Winthrop Jordan's *White Over Black*, p. 7) of how intensely blackness is hated in the "English heritage." Quoting Jordan on p. 81 of *Unmeltable Ethnics*, Novak shares the following:

In England perhaps more than in southern Europe, the concept of blackness was loaded with intense meaning. Long before they found out that some men were black, Englishmen found in the idea of blackness a way of expressing some of their most ingrained values. No other color except white conveyed so much emotional impact. As described by the *Oxford English Dictionary*, the meaning of *black* before the sixteenth century included, 'Deeply stained with dirt; soiled, dirty, foul. . . . Having dark or deadly purposes, malignant; pertaining to or involving death, deadly; baneful, disastrous, sinister. . . . Foul, iniquitous, atrocious, horrible, wicked. . . . Indicating disgrace, censure, liability to punishment, etc.' Black was an emotionally partisan color, the handmaid and symbol of baseness and evil, a sign of danger and repulsion.
  Embedded in the concept of blackness was its direct opposite—whiteness. No other colors so clearly implied opposition, 'being coloures utterlye contrary'; no others were so frequently used to denote polarization. . . . White and black connoted purity and filthiness, virginity and sin, virtue and baseness, beauty and ugliness, beneficence and evil, God and the devil.

†Novak seems to understand and not to understand the powerful influence that *being white* was (and is) in the efforts and achievements of white ethnics.

how they *as whites* (in contrast to Blacks) were received at this country's stations of opportunity, is how European immigrants willingly sought recognition as "full Americans" and so deemphasized, even stamped out, their ethnic specialness. It was the priority given to *being white* that has made white ethnics come so late to the feast of identity.*

The point here is that for white ethnics to cry about not having been recognized for their uniquely ethnic selves, after having encouraged their own homogenization with other whites—their own melting in the pot of *white* America—is a questionable position. In fact, Novak's title is not an accurate description. He really writes about the *already melted* white ethnics who are now trying to rediscover their uniqueness and variety. To counter possible questions about support for this assertion I ask the following two questions. Did mere happenstance occasion the dust jacket design for *Unmeltable Ethnics*–white printing for the word "unmeltable"? Or did the artist recognize and reveal ironically the truth that white ethnics have *already been melted* into America's cauldron of whiteness?

Whatever the answers, the dominance of whiteness over ethnicity is indicated in Novak's chapter "Confessions of a White Ethnic," where he shares his early sense of identification. He says "we" when speaking of white ethnics, but "it is not an entirely comfortable 'we,' for many ethnics have not been to college, or travelled, or shared the experiences . . . [I have] had." In contrast (as I have indicated elsewhere), most if not all Blacks, regardless of educational and cultural attainments, have "shared the experiences" of being a nigger.† Novak's discomfort is based on *class* differences; all Blacks belong to the same *caste*. For at least this important reason, therefore, Blacks could not in World Wars I and II and certainly cannot today share in the

---

*Understandably, however, being white in a country that exists by the code of white superiority would not incline one to assert a distinguishingly different attribute, lest opportunities be decreased and survival itself be threatened. Obviously, most Blacks, Chicanos, Asians, and Indians could not and cannot be *seen* as white; most non-whites have no choice about revealing our races. Ours has not been the problem of maintaining our differences against visual evidence of our "sameness," and perhaps our unambiguous status has been the less morally demanding experience.

†The best story about this truth is probably Malcolm X's about the black Ph.D. who couldn't imagine what he was called by white racists. "Nigger," exclaimed Malcolm (*The Autobiography*, p. 284).

white ethnics' reverence for the American flag—the "symbol of transcendence, human dignity, and acceptance" because personhood could be proved by "expressing willingness to die beneath those colors" (p. 65). Blacks were slaves under the flag; Blacks have been segregated in the flag-preserving but soul-killing military forces of this nation; and we live close to the time when even a Black soldier's body whose coffin had been flag-draped could not be lowered into the "for whites only" ground of some of our nation's cemeteries; recently the flag represented this nation's waging war against non-white people. Hence, while moved by Novak's reminder on p. 64 that "from 1870 until 1941 ethnics were told they were not worthy of America . . . , but they believed in the dream," I must emphasize the harsher reality: Blacks have been slaves or second-class citizens for more than three centuries, and for us America's dream and the flag's honor are yet to be fulfilled. In the words of Langston Hughes, "America never was America to me."[15]

Nor was America her ideal self to white ethnics, as Novak explains so fully—but without recognizing the primary importance of whiteness in the white ethnics' lives. It is no wonder, then, that Novak also does not understand "the absence of that sympathy for PIGS which simple human feeling might have prodded intelligence to muster, that same sympathy which the educated find so easy to conjure up for black culture, Chicano culture, Indian culture" (p. 58). There is a simple answer to Novak's question (p. 58), "Why do the educated classes find it so difficult to want to understand the man who drives a beer truck, or the fellow with a helmet working on a site across the street with plumbers and electricians?" *Caste* differences, *racial* distinctions, allow the liberals among dominant whites in the U.S.A. to maintain their illusion of superiority even while helping and sympathizing with Blacks, Chicanos, Indians, and Asians. For no one could ever confuse the helper with the needy. When confronted with disadvantaged white ethnics, however, the liberals among dominant whites are frightened by the sense of *themselves* in the PIGS. All whites are in the same caste too.* (Interestingly, an adult Margaret

---

*Instructive in this context is Morales's discussion of "consciousness of kind," quoted above. Just as we seem to harm more easily those whom we consider

Mead attributes part of her happiness to her mother's insistence
that the child call the Black servant woman "Mrs.," which was,
as Mead says, "a refusal of a caste position."[16] That is, her
caste allowed her to address the Black woman differently from
"Mrs."; her mother's fullness of humanity, however, denied
to Mead the exercise of a caste privilege.)

Blacks agree with Novak's observation (p. 115) about WASPs'
never having had to "celebrate Columbus Day or march down
Fifth Avenue wearing green. Every day has been their day
in America. No more." But we agree with a difference. Until
recently Blacks have not been able to utilize public space and
time to celebrate *any* days special to us. We have viewed Columbus Day and St. Patrick's Day as part of the larger truth that
"every day has been . . . [white folks'] day in America." And
to this historical reality Blacks also say, "No more." White ethnics
should understand how deeply ingrained they are in the white
yoke of oppression that Blacks now seek to throw off.

Although Blacks hardly seem to be his primary audience,
at least in the context of his proposal for a coalition between
Blacks and white ethnics Novak should consider the impact
of his jointly hostile and admiring attitudes upon Blacks, for
some of us are confused by his apparent ambivalence toward
us as a people. On the one hand, we applaud his proclamations
that "persons who are secure in their identity act with greater
freedom, greater flexibility, greater openness to others" (p. 9);
that "the establishment of systems of identity and self-respect
is as crucial for whites as for blacks" (p. 19); that "people uncer-
tain of their own identity are not wholly free" (p. 229). We
understand the delicacy and complexity of white ethnics' emotions regarding Blacks; we respect the honesty of admitting
that Blacks *have* suffered more. On the other hand, we wonder
about the following passage on p. 168:

> There is abroad in the land a great awe of black militance. Otherwise
> sensible men are impressed by the solidarity, discipline, anger, hatred,
> and determination on the part of radicalized blacks. No one should underes-
> timate the resources of a matching hatred and ruthlessness. *Every* ethnic

to be different from ourselves, so do we shrink from our likeness when
it is in degrading circumstances. Identification is absent from the first situation;
it is overwhelming in the second. The extension of charity and the experience
of empathy when relating to "others" or to likenesses of the self, illustrate
the dominance sometimes of these impulses over ego and pride.

group has turned to violence in order to gain a place in American life. [Here Novak refers to a note on several works that illustrate this point.] Yet people praise black violence, but not the violence of the United Mine Workers, the Teamsters, the syndicates. Someone must make the argument in America, because it is true, that black militance can push some WASPS and some liberals around, but it will *not* push ethnics around. It is essential to everybody concerned to get underlying emotions and underlying commitments straight.

We wonder also about the organization and the substance of many passages referring to Blacks in Novak's book.* We question, for example, the relevance of the passage here quoted to the argument of the chapter in which it appears, entitled "Jewish and Catholic." We note the innuendo accomplished by the juxtaposing of black militants and Al Capone in a paragraph preceding this passage (on the same page, 168). But extraordinarily curious in organization is the following paragraph (p. 78): "A man named Procaccino declared himself a candidate for mayor of New York. At a dinner in New Haven, a well-known professor said aloud: 'If Italians aren't actually an inferior race, they do the best imitation of one I've seen.'

---

*Consider the following examples of Novak's apparently ambivalent attitude toward Blacks, an ambivalence that affects his logic adversely. To be sure, the tone and texture of the book in this regard cannot be sensed fully by reading excerpts or references. One has to experience the whole book, alerted, perhaps, by these examples. (1) An opening discussion (pp. 4-5) of the political activity and subsequent shooting of Joe Colombo includes a statement that Blacks have "had heroes who had been criminals." The statement is superficial, however, in not distinguishing between the Mafia or other groups or syndicates of *organized* criminals, and black individuals who have been arrested but have not always been proven to be criminals, or whose lives illustrate a post-criminal significance (consider, e.g., Huey Newton or Bobby Seale or Angela Davis and Malcolm X or Eldridge Cleaver). This is an example of Novak's making too easy an identification between Blacks and white ethnics, as he seeks to validate the behavior of the latter. (2) On pp. 6-7 Novak reveals his understanding of the inherent racism of "social issue" and "law and order" politics, and on p. 13 and elsewhere he reports complete agreement among white ethnics that "blacks get the worse deal in American life." However, Novak does not question the related erroneous assumption by white ethnics that "the gains of blacks . . . [are] solely at *their* expense" (p. 14). (3) Novak implies in many passages (pp. 58, 61, 78, and 142 are mentioned in this paper) that Blacks and other non-whites are responsible for the behavior and attitudes of dominant whites toward white ethnics. (4) There is an unsupported suggestion on p. 240 (in the context of a critique of government policies that drove folk from rural to urban areas) that during the last thirty years immigration to American cities has meant a majority of Blacks on urban welfare rolls and that a twenty-percent increase in urban black populations

Everyone at the table laughed. The professor didn't make that kind of joke when Bobby Seale was on trial." The passage seems to imply that because he is black and was on trial, Bobby Seale might have deserved to be the butt of "that kind of joke." But why a reference to Seale and a trial in this context? Is Seale to be blamed for the professor's comments? Novak quotes (p. 60) a Chicago white ethnic who says, "we're the new invisible man, the new whipping boy," but these passages and others in *The Rise of the Unmeltable Ethnics* say clearly to Blacks that *we* are still it—the winner and champion of white people's hatred.

White Ethnics, Black Protestants, and the Challenge

With regard to the sharp differences between Catholic and Protestant views of the world and of self, Novak errs in generalizing about Protestants without any qualifying observations on black Protestants. He has not observed, for example, that the survival needs and many cultural aspects of being black in this country have created in Blacks much that he praises or understands as inevitable in white ethnics: experiencing religion as "a way of feeling, an attitude, a sentiment" (p. 208); "an instinct for family and community" (p. 209); a "preoccupation with

is of itself a problem. (5) Generalizing on pp. 254-55 about cultural (not racial or color) contrasts between Slavic and black culture, Novak (notwithstanding an awkwardly attached qualification) imputes to Blacks a characteristic of "conspicuous consumption" of which Slavs are said to be contemptuous. (6) Ascribing to white ethnics and Blacks dissimilar attitudes "toward family values," Novak makes (on p. 255) one of the most uncritical statements in the book: "The black family seems to be more like the modern liberal family in respect to its sexual mores." What evidence supports "seems"? What does Novak mean? The glibness merely compounds a large error.

With regard to example 5 in this note, Novak does not understand that cultural habits are not the issue. For in a society that has whiteness or being "white" as its highest value, "white" members of the society will be free to cultivate inconspicuous styles while still maintaining—without conscious effort—their *basic* worth and reason for pride. Unliberated Black members of the society will try to acquire highly visible material goods in substitution for the unattainable most worthy characteristic—a "white" skin. Not even to hint at this important historical and psychological reality while purporting to discuss cultural differences is to present uncritical descriptions and value judgments as if they were truth. Unless *white racism* is recognized as basic to all cultural patterns in the U.S.A., we speak idly about cultural conflicts. (Although narrow in focus, a very instructive work about self-esteem and styles among Blacks is Joyce A. Ladner's work *Tomorrow's Tomorrow: The Black Woman* (Garden City, N.Y., 1972), especially pp. 80-81 and 122-24.

economic necessities" (p. 218); workers' placing high value on "strong leadership, personal services, a minimum of theoretical discussion or intellectual debate" (p. 226). More accurate than to lump Blacks with Protestants* would be to observe in Blacks the *combining* of rational and visceral responses to the world.

That is, while they share with other Protestants the tendency "to test the quality of religious life by the propriety of one's deeds" (p. 208), by emphasizing the repentance and forgiving aspects of the New Testament, black Protestants have *not* become moralistic and austerely ethical to the exclusion of gut-level responses to the concepts of right and wrong and an understanding of human frailty. And so—to take the most extreme, perhaps, but historically constant example—no matter what the longing for circumstances to have been otherwise, black Protestants have usually supported unwed mothers-to-be; have usually kept and loved the children—even the half-whites—that the dominant society labels as bastards; and have usually made "family" mean *all* who are part of ourselves.[17] In contrast, white Protestants have frequently rejected unwed mothers-to-be or aborted the fetuses or forced the mothers to give up their children; and white Protestant fathers of partly black children have most frequently not only closed the doors of family to such children, but have often also denied their offspring's humanity by enslaving and otherwise brutalizing them.

This different response by whites to new life (that is, the requirement that it be "legitimate" and "white" in order, perhaps, to be accepted or loved) parallels what I see as the basic problem in white-black relationships in the U.S.A. Whites have not been able to accept or identify with the totality of human life represented in our society, because they place a false value on a single attribute: skin color, or, more accurately, race.

In the context of such false valuation—were one to recognize it—merely to confirm that "life . . . is suffering" (as Novak does on p. 208) and to emphasize God's revelation in Jesus as "suffering love" are not enough. To be acknowledged and understood are the *extra* burdens, the *extra* suffering, imposed by racism; else one seems to dismiss casually a basically human

*That is, were Novak to give serious consideration to Blacks as Protestants, instead of merely referring (as he does on p. 12) to the religious heritage shared by Martin Luther King, Jr., and Southern white Protestants.

claim to justice. As James Baldwin said to Margaret Mead, "The price [suffering] one pays is everybody's price. But on top of that particular price, which is universal, there is something gratuitous which I will not forgive, you know. It's difficult to be born, difficult to learn to walk, difficult to grow old, difficult to die and difficult to live for everybody, everywhere, forever. But no one has a right to put on top of that another burden, another price which nobody can pay, and a burden which really nobody can bear."[18]

Baldwin's points are crucial to understanding a black person's responses to the rise of white ethnicity. Black history in this country is a story of denial in its extremity. Because of our acute and prolonged suffering, we Blacks *do* empathize with others who suffer. But we refuse to grant primacy to the needs of white people who have required of us that gratuitous price. The suffering of *all* or the end of *all* oppression are the alternative courses that some Blacks see for this nation. In other words, if our society cannot or does not want to solve the problems of suffering related to racism, then *let us all die* in our polluted air; let us blow up the *whole* earth; let us end *human* life.* For existence in an unjust world that requires all to suffer is one thing†; to endure the *special* injustice and consequent suffering of racism is another. That is the price that Blacks will no longer pay.

Therefore, while I join Novak in his pleas to *all* ethnics to unite and for all people to establish our identities and to respect the identities of each other, I must proclaim still what I see as a prerequisite for such union: In the U.S.A. whites will have to learn to see themselves—their "me"—in black selves, the hardly acknowledged "thee" of the extreme other. Whites will have to see in their black compatriots a confirmation of their

---

*Although superbly practical, the point of John B. Cobb's allegory (in *Is It Too Late? A Theology of Ecology*, Beverly Hills, Cal., 1972, pp. 13-17) is that, once again, Blacks and all other oppressed people should join in "human" efforts—this time to prevent the earth's destruction by pollution. Cobb argues that *life* itself is threatened and that the preservation of life is *the* issue. Many Blacks in this *country*, however, think that the *quality* of life for all people must be more than arbitrarily determined and that a *good life for all* or *no life for any* are the only options left.

†Novak observes correctly on p. 239 that the U.S.A. (unlike a Catholic society) is not a country that stresses "the common hard lot of all, and the common grace."

own humanity, whether joyful or sorrowful. Whites will have to *transcend their whiteness as a primary value*, as an attribute of superiority, before they can *rediscover* and fulfill the promises of their *ethnic* uniqueness. "To see the me in thee"—this is the challenge from Blacks to *all* whites in America. Are you listening, ethnic Americans? Do PIGS have ears?*

NOTES

1. George Henry Lewes, as quoted by Franklin Henry Giddings, *The Principles of Sociology* (New York, 1896), pp. 132-33, cited in Armando Morales, "The Collective Preconscious and Racism," *Social Casework*, 52 (May 1971), 287.
2. Morales, p. 287, citing p. 18 of Giddings' work (italics added).
3. Charles A. Reich, *The Greening of America* (New York, 1970), pp. 164, 366-67.
4. See, e.g., "The New Minority" (editorial), *America*, 123 (October 10, 1970), 253, and two articles by Thomas H. Clancy, "The Ethnic American—An Interview with Barbara Mikulski," *America*, 123 (December 26, 1970), 558, and "Ethnic Consciousness I," *America*, 124 (January 9, 1971), 10.
5. Blacks in the labor market and in labor unions are discussed in all the general histories of Blacks in the U.S.A. See John Hope Franklin, *From Slavery to Freedom: A History of Negro Americans*, 3rd edition (New York, 1969); Saunders Redding, *They Came in Chains: Americans from Africa* (1950, reprinted New York, 1969); Drake and Cayton, *Black Metropolis,* especially chapters 9-12, Arna Bontemps and Jack Conroy, *Anyplace But Here* (1945 [with the title *They Seek A City*], reprinted New York, 1966), share instructive vignettes of Blacks in the labor market.
6. "Blacks and Organized Labor," *Black Enterprise*, 2 (July 1972), 16-18, 20-21, 49.
7. Clancy, "The Ethnic American—An Interview with Barbara Mikulski," p. 559.
8. Bontemps and Conroy, p. 144. See also Franklin's comments in the note on p. 24 above, as well as Redding, p. 279.
9. Novak, pp. 24-28, 30, 228.
10. The passage is cited by Novak at the start of part two of *The Rise of the Unmeltable Ethnics*.
11. Malcolm X (with Alex Haley), *The Autobiography of Malcolm X* (New York, 1965), p. 285.

*Most readers know that in current discussions of white ethnicity, at least since Novak, *PIGS* is the acronym for Poles, Italians, Greeks, and Slavs and an inclusive term for all white ethnics. It is to be distinguished, of course, from "Pigs," an also current pejorative metaphor among many young Blacks and liberal white college youth for policemen and secret agents. (Considering the ethnic backgrounds of many of the nation's city policemen, however, PIGS and Pigs may be more closely related than at first recognized.)

12. "Ethnic Consciousness I," *America*, 124 (January 9, 1971), 10.

13. Mike Royko, *Boss* (New York, 1971), p. 25, quoted in Novak, *Unmeltable Ethnics*, pp. 11-12.

14. Novak, *Unmeltable Ethnics*, pp. 8, 30-31, 58, 61, and elsewhere.

15. "Let America Be America Again," *Esquire, The Magazine for Men*, 6 (July 1936), 92.

16. Margaret Mead and James Baldwin, *A Rap on Race* (1971; reprinted New York, 1972), p. 219.

17. This subject is discussed fully by Ladner in *Tomorrow's Tomorrow*: see especially pp. 165-66, 199-221, 229-33, and sections on contraception (pp. 247-56) and on abortion (pp. 256-63).

18. *A Rap on Race*, p. 256.

SOCIOLOGICAL PERSPECTIVES
ON THE STRANGER

EDWARD A. TIRYAKIAN

> I don't know any strangers—just friends I haven't met yet.
>
> Jennie Grossinger

BY WAY OF PREFACE, it should be noted that in the mainstream corpus of sociological literature the significance of the stranger has been of residual interest. For the most part, sociologists have been dealing with modern Western societies, characterized by complexity of social organization, heterogeneity of populations, and an extensive level of urbanization. Since urban areas have tended to recruit their population from the outside (from outlying rural areas, regions, and even from other countries), modern societies have such a high proportion of "strangers" that the ubiquity of the latter may in itself be a reason why they have been overlooked by sociologists. On the other hand, anthropologists have tended to focus by and large on relatively homogeneous "folk" societies tacitly taken to be isolated from processes of historical change[1]; strangers in such societies are rare and marginal. Hence the anthropological literature is as sparse on the significance of the stranger as is the sociological, though the fact that the anthropologist going into the field is himself a stranger could greatly enhance our understanding of the stranger's perspective on social reality, if that fact were fully realized and exploited in self-reflection

Mr. Tiryakian, who has taught at Princeton and at Harvard, is presently on the Sociology faculty at Duke University. His major interests are sociological theory and the sociology of religion.

by anthropologists.* The social science literature on the stranger has illuminated many aspects of the meaning of the stranger to a host group, but the perception of the host group by the stranger remains pretty much an untrodden field.

In the present article I shall draw from some of the more important complementary pieces in the sociological and anthropological literature, but my major concern will be to indicate to the reader broader, qualitative dimensions of social life which stem from a consideration of "the stranger." In particular I hope to draw attention to structural and dynamic considerations of the polarity of the familiar and the strange which are brought into relief by the presence of the stranger in the host (and often hostile) group.

The sociological awareness of the stranger traces back to a seminal piece of Georg Simmel.† Simmel (himself something of a stranger in his own terms to the German academic world) treated the stranger as a potential wanderer who is marginal to a group because he does not belong to the group yet contributes to its existence by his presence; he is outside the group and yet confronts it. Not grounded in the group's traditional kinship or political structures, the stranger is more mobile than other group members and more objective about the group's way of life. Bound by no commitments to the existent way of life, the stranger in his objectivity is more free to perceive things as they are than are group members whose perspectives are more partial. The stranger's objectivity, suggested Simmel, makes him both near and far to others; one relates to the stranger in terms of only general qualities of human nature.

---

*Thomas Beidelman has drawn attention to the "involuntary alienation" of the anthropologist as a source of enrichment in his understanding of both his own society and the society in which he is a temporary stranger. See his article, "Some Sociological Implications of Culture," in John C. McKinney and Edward A. Tiryakian, eds., *Theoretical Sociology: Perspectives and Developments* (New York, 1970).

†Georg Simmel, "The Stranger," in Kurt Wolff, tr. and ed., *The Sociology of Georg Simmel* (New York, 1950), pp. 402-08. This was first published in German in 1908, and first translated into English by Robert E. Park in 1921. Park and his student E.V. Stonequist expanded Simmel's concept of the stranger into a better-known one, that of the "marginal man," a bearer of cultural change. The two concepts overlap but are not identical. See Everett V. Stonequist, *The Marginal Man* (New York, 1937).

Thus, by implication, the stranger has a greater freedom than others, a freedom bestowed upon him by his objectivity and mobility. And this also entails that one can be freer with a stranger than with social familiars, with persons one knows intimately. The stranger, because of his transience and his anonymity (the stranger is the unknown other), can receive confidences which we would be reticent to divulge to those who know us and who form part of our everyday social world.

Simmel pointed out that the stranger is a mediating figure between the near and the far. In many societies it is strangers or stranger groups who are the traders bringing in goods from the outside and taking others out. Since the stranger is not attached to the soil, he has the mobility which permits him to come and go as a trader. But the mobility of the stranger entails a broader social role than just an economic one, since the stranger can interact with anyone in the social hierarchy or social structure, whether or not his entry into the host society stems from economic exchanges. Simmel's observation on this score has ample verification. The anthropologist who goes to a small isolated community can find out how the total community is organized (and divided) through getting the confidence of all sides; while the members have a well-defined social identity anchored in one subgrouping of the total community, the anthropologist qua stranger is not identified as belonging to one faction. This can extend even to the sociologist who visits a more culturally complex society marked by a cleavage in its population. I have here in mind the striking experience of Renée Fox, a sociologist who went a few years ago to study the organization of Belgian medical schools. The French-speaking and the Flemish-speaking medical faculties lived in virtual isolation and ignorance of each other; as a stranger she found out about both and became an important source of knowledge about the doings of each community to the other.[2]

If being a stranger grants one a certain ease to roam about in the social structure, it also imposes restrictions on his movement. The stranger as such is an intrusion and an intruder; this is a fundamental determination of his social relationship. He not only intrudes on the familiar, on the taken-for-granted ground of everyday life; because of his intrusion he makes us conscious of the familiar by representing another realm of social reality "out there" which is unfamiliar and strange. The stranger, then, is crucial in introducing into our awareness the polarity of "inside" and "outside," for he is a representative of the "outside" to "insiders"; by his presence he is a challenger to insiders' social organization, to their way of life, to their assumptions about social reality.

The stranger is not a social nonentity; by bringing the unknown into our sphere of perception he receives a social identity of prime significance. As the embodiment of the foreign, the social perception of the stranger is characterized by *ambiguity*; the feelings he evokes, by a complex ambivalence. Let us elaborate on this formulation.

As a bearer of the strange, the foreign, the unknown, the stranger as the knower and participant in the unfamiliar has an immediate authority in comparison to "locals" ignorant of the outside. His familiarity with the unfamiliar gives him a certain power and authority. The stranger's social role in this context has a seductive quality which makes his person a source of attraction. What is strange is in and of itself novel, and the new is exciting precisely because it is the unexperienced. But at the same time, the not yet experienced is also threatening and unsettling. The stranger as the bearer of the strange is also the person who can unhinge the familiar, the person who as a representative of the strange has powers not available to "locals"; he is a potential disorganizer of the familiar, one who can turn things or the order of things "inside out." Hence the stranger is not only highly welcome; he is also highly unwelcome. He both relieves the monotony of the everyday social setting and places it in jeopardy by his presence. The "stranger at the gate" (a recurrent title in fiction and non-fiction) is in every case the one whose coming places in question the community's existence; his knock is that of an outside social reality which suddenly impinges on the group and places its existence (and survival) in question. In a sense we can say that the stranger qua foreigner presents a test of the community's self-confidence about its existence.

The responses to the stranger's knock are varied. It is not overly facile to say that the evidence shows a historical trend in attitudes toward strangers as societies have evolved from closed small communities toward relatively open and complex societies.[3]

In ancient societies, the stranger typically had the status of being the one without a civil status, without the civil rights common to the members of the community; he was the intruder, the alien. Seen as or equated with the enemy, suspected of bringing with him hostile spirits, the stranger is here experienced as a source of potential disorder and confusion who must either be exterminated on the spot or be treated with extreme caution, which may take the form of politeness and deference. In the latter instance it is the stranger who benefits from the convention of hospitality.

Few societies have gone as far in incorporating into their religion the stranger element as did the ancient Egyptians, who made an important place for the worship of Seth, the foreign god; when relationships between Egypt and stranger groups (Persians, Assyrians, Semites) became strained and hostile, Seth was downgraded in the Egyptian pantheon.[4] But since early societies did not differentiate between religious and social organization (i.e., religious organization was integral to social organization), the stranger's social status had a religious significance even outside Egypt: the stranger was one who did not or was not allowed to participate fully in the religious rituals of the community, no matter how accepted he might be in other respects.* One last consideration of the religious aspect of the stranger is worth noting in this vein. Common to the Judaic, Greek, and Christian traditions is the notion of the stranger as the visiting God or his representative (e.g., an angel) who puts on a temporary cloak of anonymity. It is perhaps this possibility which makes deference and hospitality to strangers a positive prescription, counterbalancing the image of the stranger as a representative of hostile and threatening outside forces.

I have so far touched upon the complex attitudes towards the stranger, a discussion which stems from the early essay of Simmel and from a later phenomenological amplification by Alfred Schutz.[5] But a sociological perspective on the stranger

*Thus the ancient Jews recognized several categories of strangers: *zarim* and *nokhrim* designated peripheral foreigners or outsiders; the *ger* was a resident alien who enjoyed protection (including protection from usury) because he could participate in some rituals insofar as he was a proselyte; the *ger toshav* was the non-Jew living as a settled resident who accepted some but not all of the commandments of the Torah. For an elaboration of types, see "Strangers" in the *Encyclopedia Judaica*, vol. 15 (New York, 1971), 419-21.

has also to be based on structural considerations, that is, the structural position of strangers in the societal setting in which they are found, including changes in the definition of their position in the social structure. It is at this point that we can expand our notion from the stranger as a person to the stranger as a grouping of outsiders cohabitating with indigenes, with "natives," those born in and of the land.

The study of the relation of stranger groups to a host society owes much to Max Weber's economic sociology. Although he did not explicitly refer to strangers, he implicitly did so in his notion of a "pariah people." In distinguishing pariah capitalism from modern capitalism, Weber[6] drew attention to social groups acting chiefly as traders (e.g., Jews in the West, Parsees in India) rather than economic innovators; such groups are marginal to the society where they exist, forming essentially a despised and set apart "pariah" caste whose situation is always to some extent precarious. At the same time they are tolerated because of their economic services and may even enjoy special privileges. In his discussion, Weber made a brief mention of the importance of territoriality: a group that loses political autonomy and is forced to live in a "diaspora" may become a pariah or "guest" people (as in the case of Jews, Armenians, and slaves brought to the Western hemisphere from Africa). From this we can suggest that the mobility, voluntary or involuntary, of a stranger group is, at least in part, a function of the absence of a definite territoriality.

Stranger groups (rather than individual strangers) have been a noted social presence in many areas of the world, not just the West (where the Jew has been a sort of archetypal figure of the stranger). The case of Africa is illustrative of this. The anthropologist Elliot Skinner, in discussing West African societies, has added to the image of the stranger drawn from Simmel and Weber by giving emphasis to the changing status of the stranger as a function of changes in the larger socio-cultural system of the host society.[7] An important factor in changes in the status and role of stranger groups was the imposition of colonialism onto traditional African society. Traditional West African societies had their stranger groups, predominantly merchants and traders, living in their own residential quarters in African urban and political centers. Their numbers were small as a percentage of the total population, and there was no question that they were subordinated to the local African political authorities. They did not have the same political rights and obligations as the indigenes, though, as elsewhere in the world where stranger groups lived in residentially segregated zones, they customarily policed their own internal affairs.

African colonial society brought about some far-reaching changes with regard to strangers; it also led to changes in the political relationships of stranger groups to the host African community. Thus in West Africa the colonial powers brought in or encouraged the immigration of large numbers of Levantines, who became important small-scale capitalists (of the pariah capitalism sort described by Weber). In East Africa and in South Africa, large numbers of Asiatics (chiefly from India) came originally as railway workers or sugar cane cutters and then became middle men in trade or lower-rung civil servants. The colonial system also encouraged, directly or indirectly, the influx of new African strangers through the political realignment of African territories (for example, the integration of Nigeria as a colony led to the influx of Ibos in the North).

Skinner points out that these "new" strangers, whether Africans or non-Africans, had their political allegiance not to traditional local African authorities but to colonial authorities. In the colonial society they were frequently a buffer or intermediary group between the indigenes and colonial authorities.[8] Their marginality—a feature common to any stranger group—was both an asset and a liability. An asset, for in the colonial regime they were important adjuncts of the colonial system; often they spoke the language of the colonizer and had relatively greater familiarity with his culture than the "natives." But their very existence as an adjunct of the colonial system was also for these stranger groups a liability. With independence the withdrawal of colonial authorities also meant that the socio-economic status of stranger groups became more visible and relatively more elevated. Hence stranger groups became the object of envy and aggression. Even if in the period preceding independence they had been in alliance with nationalistic movements, after independence stranger groups lacked political protection and were more likely to be seen as enemies and exploiters of the people than as part of the new national community. The examples in the past ten or fifteen years of Dahomeyans in the Ivory Coast, Levantines in Mali, and Asiatics in East Africa (witness the recent mass expulsion of Indians from Uganda) attest to the unstable and precarious situation of stranger groups.

Although Skinner does not mention this, it might be pointed out that not only did the colonial regime bring in new strangers, but new strangers in some instances were also the harbinger of a coming colonial regime. Thus in South Africa nearly a century ago the "Uitlanders" who flocked to the Transvaal gold fields became, because of their political disenfranchisement in the Boer republic, a pretext for British imperialism seeking to justify the annexation of the Transvaal. And Elspeth Huxley in her sensitive novel *Red Strangers*[9] makes very vivid how (in the context of Kenya) the new strangers were not just newcomers but intruders who effected permanent changes as agents of colonization.

Stranger groups, as this brief discussion of the African colonial setting may serve to indicate, occupy a temporary relationship since they lack roots or anchor in the soil. They may become expelled or (as in the case of the Highlands of Kenya) they may become the expellers. On a short-term basis, the strangers as intermediaries can occupy an advantageous buffer position, but their political vulnerability has long-term disadvantages, especially in any period in which the host society undergoes strong nationalistic feelings and movements. A nationalistic movement, whether its political basis is from the right or the left, fundamentally involves a purification of the body politic which is viewed as having been contaminated by external, non-indigenous forces and agents; in such a tightening of the criteria of in-group membership, strangers as representatives of the outside become a target for exclusion. The stranger ultimately cannot identify with "national" interests; he is suspect of being antinational precisely because he is "alien." In the formative years of the American republic, when the problem of defining the national community was still acute, legislation against "aliens," though it was short-lived, reflected nationalistic senti-ments against outsiders. Even Russia in the 1920's, during the formative years of the Soviet regime which saw itself as the embodiment of world-wide socialist revolution, could not toler-ate Trotskyites, who were denounced as "rootless   cos-mopolitans" by the Stalinists—and "rootless cosmopolitans" is certainly a typification (if not a vilification) of the stranger or stranger groups as such.

We started this paper by discussing elements of how the stranger is perceived. The discussion of stranger groups in colonial and post-colonial settings introduced the fact that the status of stranger groups is subject to change along with the socio-political setting of the host country. There is another aspect to colonization which is pertinent for expanding our perspective on the psycho-social dimensions of the stranger and the strange. "Stranger" is not a static category of social being; it is a social category that any one or any social group may move into and out of, most typically by wandering or migrating from the familiar setting of home to the distant, the unfamiliar. But colonization also produces a different kind of strangers, those who have become strangers in their own land.

Colonization, however varied its historical manifestations, involves the coming of a stranger group having technological superiority (including weaponry) and able to become "masters" over the native population. Whether the native population is driven off the land which was its home (as in the case, most notably, of the American Indians) or allowed to remain on the land in a subordinated economic and political status (as in the case of India, North Africa, and most of sub-Sahara Africa), its traditional culture becomes demeaned, invalidated, suppressed, or driven underground. Particularly in the case of modern colonization, the native population comes to be *estranged* from its own cultural roots; what was formerly "home" becomes the "strange," at least for those members of the indigenes who come to participate in the cultural system of the colonial system.* Seen from this perspective, colonization is a process of self-estrangement, an alienative process wherein

---

*How this is done involves complex mechanisms of "assimilation." Western-style education has been a major vehicle of assimilation and at the same time of alienation in the sense of estrangement from one's culture. The testimony of E.B. Rugumayo, Uganda's Minister of Education, is eloquent in this context: "I was brought up under a colonial system of education . . . In my time I learnt about the history, geography, songs, poetry and even science of England . . . I had to adopt a non-African name as a passport to heaven. The local songs and the religions of the areas were literally banned as being unsuitable. Certain attitudes were engendered, thus producing a particular type of individual—an individual who is ashamed of his own culture . . . ("Education for Character Training," *Mawazo*, 3 [June, 1972], 14.

outside strangers bring into being a group of "new strangers" by alienating them from their own culture and people. Once there is a recognition of this estrangement in the form of independence movements, those who continue to associate or identify with the outside strangers become themselves the object of moral outrage, often being singled out for extremes of physical violence (thus the F.L.N. and the Mau Mau took the lives of more Algerians and Kikuyu than they did of French colons and English settlers).

The complexity of the stranger-host relationship is not confined to primitive, early, or even colonial society. The fullness of the social significance of the stranger becomes manifest most markedly when we turn our attention to modern Western society. This society, which we take as home and the familiar, is also one characterized by the amalgam of stranger groups and by the formation of stranger groups on such a massive scale that upon reflection it may not be far-fetched to label the typical national community of Western society as more "a nation of strangers"[10] than a national unity.

In nineteenth-century Europe the urban-industrial order brought about vast social transformations and dislocations of traditional communities, with one concomitant being a very sharp differentiation of the population, particularly the differentiation of the new middle classes from the new working classes. This hiatus formed the heart of the "social question," of major concern to radicals, reformers, and conservatives alike. As early as 1845 the conservative reformer Benjamin Disraeli had pointed out in his social novel, *Sybil or the Two Nations*, the great gulf separating the two new great social classes of Wealth and Work who lacked sympathy for one another because of mutual ignorance. Disraeli's message was that modern society could not achieve its potential for national prosperity until the two ceased being strangers to one another (and he hoped that the House of Commons would assume a leadership role in mediating between the two stranger groups).

It would be beside the point to evaluate Disraeli's remedy in comparison to other observers sensitive to the "social question" such as Marx on the one hand and Durkheim on the other. More pertinent is that Disraeli's "discovery" of strangers in the midst of modern society was to be a repeated experience on both sides of the Atlantic Ocean. Thus the astonishment of middle-class Englishmen seventy years ago at the findings of Charles Booth's monumental seventeen-volume survey of London,[11] which revealed great pockets of poverty embracing nearly one-third of London's inhabitants, is strikingly similar to middle-class America's recent "discovery" of the presence of poverty in our metropolitan centers: then as now the poor form a stranger class, even if the poor today are not only economically differentiated but also racially and ethnically differentiated. And then as now one reaction of the middle class has been to increase the spatial distance between itself and the stranger group,* which for those concerned with national integration cannot simply be dismissed as an archetypal reaction of fleeing from the "pariahs" because these are seen as a source of pollution. Disraeli's problem is still our problem.

A further characteristic of American society which bears on our discussion is the salience of mobility, both geographical and social; the extent of mobility means that every year millions of persons in the United States experience becoming strangers in leaving the familiar community for the unfamiliar.† Much of the mobility has been a constant structure in the American scene, from the very dawn of our society's coming into being. But in the past twenty years structural changes have added to our traditional mobility, changes which have brought about new groups as strangers. Ethnic and religious enclaves have broken down from pressures both within and without, and one result has been that ethnic, racial, and religious minorities in the last twenty years have experienced becoming strangers by moving into formerly strange and alien territory. A great many Catholics who formerly attended Catholic campuses have

---

*Note the contemporaneity of Booth's observation: "One of the dangers of the growth of London, as we have seen in happen, is the tendency for the better-to-do classes to fly the furtherest off, centrifugally, with the result that residential London tends to be arranged by class in rings with the most uniform poverty at the centre" (*Life and Labour*, Final Volume, p. 205).

†To make this more precise, out of a population of nearly 197 million as of March 1969, 18 percent had been living at a different address the year before. In different terms, 23 million Americans moved within counties, 6.3 millions within the same State, and 6.6 millions crossed state lines. For greater information, see U.S. Department of Commerce, *Population Characteristics*, Series P-20, No. 193, December 26, 1969. In terms of the previous twenty years this was a normal rather than an unusual percentage.

become temporary strangers in going to non-Catholic colleges and universities, and the traumatic experience of leaving "home" for an "alien" setting has been even more vividly experienced by Black students going to white universities.

The breakdown of segregation walls, while renovating the American commitment to democracy, has not solved the problem of stranger groups; it has made the problem more visible and acute. The dissolution of the culture of stranger groups, no matter how partial, also implies the problem of reconstructing a national culture, a set of expressive symbols providing meaning for an enlarged and more heterogeneous social community. And an enlarged culture today cannot simply be the culture of the formerly politically-dominant "host" group. White Anglo-Saxon Protestants seem no longer to be accepted as the majority group whose culture served in the past as host for minority groups; they are now themselves talked about as one ethnic group among many. It is not far-fetched to suggest that for many White Anglo-Saxon Protestants (not that this group ever had the ethnic and cultural homogeneity ascribed to it by the pejorative labelling of "WASP"), their displacement is making them feel like "aliens" in their own land, just as some white political radicals feel that the present social order of the United States is in "alien" rule—hence the reference of the latter to this state of affairs in terms of a Kafka-like usage of "Amerika" to denote *their* estrangement. And finally, the rise of the "Third World" movement in the United States (notably among Blacks, Indians, and Hispano-Americans) also reflects the self-conscious estrangement of a significant segment of the population from feeling at home in the United States.

These remarks have been made to propose that a sociological perspective on the stranger must take into account the dynamic aspect of the concept, that is, the processual aspect of the relationship of stranger and host. One can *become* a stranger to others and for others, and one can become estranged from one's self and one's milieu; conversely, strangers to one another can become familiar. Social life is punctuated by these reciprocal processes: just as physical disasters typically lead the survivors to stop being strangers unto one another, at least during the immediate post-disaster period, so also, on the other hand, do persons become strangers to one another where formerly there was a community, all the way from marriage partners to large social segments, such as generations, and even, in the case of civil wars, large territorial regions.

It is here, with the dynamics and dialectics of the stranger role, that we have a great need for additional reflection and research. Tacitly the literature on the stranger, whether it be from fiction, from sociology, or from anthropology, has viewed him as an external given, as the other. But if the other is the stranger to the self, so also is the self a stranger to the other, or so also is the familiar world of the self a strange world. Rather than take the stranger as a given, so to speak, our perspective can be greatly enlarged by empirical research on the interaction between strangers, on the one hand, and on the other by viewing our own modern society from the perspective of stranger groups within our own society.

CONCLUSION

In the course of this article I have sought to indicate the singular importance of the stranger, and relationships to strangers, in the understanding of social reality. At the interpersonal level the stranger is par excellence the other, the non-self, who makes us aware of ourselves by indicating the boundaries of selfhood. The stranger brings us into contact with the limits of ourselves; he is a figure of fascination because he reveals to us what lies beyond the familiar. At the collective level, stranger groups constitute the same challenge to the organized community. Whether the latter broadens its horizon and its basis of organization, or whether it rejects stranger-groups, it is in the presence of stranger groups that the organized community is forced to a higher level of self-consciousness than would be the case without their presence.

Modern society may increasingly develop an ideology of universalism, tolerance, brotherhood, egalitarianism, and the like, which taken together is an aspiration to abolish the sociological category of stranger. At the same time, modern society has countervailing structural conditions which make for the creation of new stranger-relationships: increased mobility, nationalistic reactions to economic and political imperialism, socio-economic differentiation arising from technological developments (in both capitalistic or socialist regimes), internal migration of ethnic and racial groups, and so forth. From this consideration we are led to the conclusion that strangers will always be in our midst, albeit today's strangers will become tomorrow's family and today's familiars may become tomorrow's strangers. After all, social reality is stranger than fiction.

NOTES

1. A recent volume giving centrality to historical change in anthropological analysis is Victor Turner, ed., *Colonialism in Africa 1870-1960*, vol. III, *Profiles of Change: African Society and Colonial Rule* (Cambridge, 1971).
2. For an account of her experiences, see Renée C. Fox, "An American Sociologist in the Land of Belgian Medical Research," in Phillip E. Hammond, ed., *Sociologists at Work* (New York, 1964), pp. 345-91.
3. Julian L. Greifer, "Attitudes to the Stranger," *American Sociological Review*, 10 (December, 1945), 739-46.
4. See H. te Velde, *Seth, God of Confusion* (Leiden, 1967), esp. Chapter 5 ("Seth the Foreigner"), pp. 109-151.
5. Alfred Schutz, "The Stranger: An Essay in Social Psychology," in his *Collected Papers*, vol. II, ed. Arvid Brodersen (The Hague, 1964), pp. 91-105.
6. In Hans Gerth and C. Wright Mills, eds., *From Max Weber: Essays in Sociology* (New York, 1958), pp. 189f.
7. Elliott P. Skinner, "Strangers in West African Societies," *Africa*, 33 (October, 1963), 307-320.
8. For comparative materials on the buffer role of strangers in Eastern Nigeria and Eastern Uganda, see William J. and Judith L. Hanna, "The Political Structure of Urban-Centered African Communities," in Horace Miner, ed., *The City in Modern Africa* (New York, 1967), pp. 151-84.
9. New York, 1939.
10. A recent treatment of this theme is Vance Packard, *A Nation of Strangers* (New York, 1972).
11. *Life and Labour of the People in London* (London, 1902).

SELECT BIBLIOGRAPHY

1. Greifer, Julian L., "Attitudes to the Stranger," *American Sociological Review*, 10 (December 1945), 739-746.
2. Hamilton-Grierson, P.J., "Strangers," *Encyclopedia of Religion and Ethics*, vol. XI. Edinburgh: T & T Clark, 1920, pp. 883-896.
3. Meyer, Julie, "The Stranger and the City," *American Journal of Sociology*, 56 (March, 1951), 476-483.
4. Park, Robert E. and Ernest W. Burgess, *Introduction to the Science of Society*, 2nd ed. Chicago: University of Chicago Press, 1924, pp. 317-327.
5. Plotnicov, Leonard, *Strangers to the City: Urban Man in Jos, Nigeria*, Pittsburgh: University of Pittsburgh Press, 1967.
6. Schutz, Alfred, "The Stranger: An Essay in Social Psychology" in Schutz, *Collected Papers*, vol. II, ed. Arvid Brodersen. The Hague: Martinus Nijhoff, 1964, pp. 91-105. First published in 1944.
7. Simmel, Georg, "The Stranger" in Kurt H. Wolff, tr. and ed., *The Sociology of Georg Simmel*. New York: Free Press, 1950, pp. 402-08.
8. Skinner, Elliott P., "Strangers in West African Societies," *Africa*, 33 (October, 1963), 307-320.
9. Williams, Robin M., *Strangers Next Door: Ethnic Relations in American Communities*. Englewood Cliffs, N. J.: Prentice-Hall, 1964.
10. Wood, Margaret M., *The Stranger: A Study in Social Relationship*. New York: Columbia University Press, 1934.

THE REDISCOVERY OF ETHNICITY BY AMERICAN RADICALISM

WILLIAM J. PARENTE

IT IS EVIDENT that ethnicity has "arrived" in America. The intellectuals plan special issues of their journals about the subject; H.E.W. and N.E.H. lure universities into establishing programs in ethnic studies; television networks create Polish insurance investigators, black teachers, and Appalachian families; little girls tramp to school with "Kiss Me, I'm Italian" buttons on their blouses.

What is of most interest to us here is the political use of the new ethnicity. The purpose of this essay is to suggest that as a people we harbor two misconceptions about it: first, that ethnicity must necessarily be a phenomenon of the Right, and second, that it has been only recently discovered in American political life. In this brief survey I would like to focus on the continuities of radical ethnic politics in our national history.

Is the new ethnicity really "new"? Is it recently "discovered" or only "rediscovered"? Indeed, has it ever been far from the political consciousness of our people? It may be that the contemporary "backlash" of urbanized East- and South-European immigrant groups is only a continuation of the kind of resentment felt by rural Anglo-Saxons who formed the Ku Klux Klan as far back as the early Reconstruction Period.[1] In this sense, American consciousness of white ethnicity has long been with us. The busing struggle merely continues the long-interrupted enfranchisement of the slaves.

Mr. Parente, Dean of the College of Arts and Sciences and Associate Professor of Political Science at the University of Scranton, regularly teaches a course on the politics of race. His essays have appeared in *Antioch Review*, *Midstream*, *America*, and the *New York Times*, among other publications.

There is, additionally, considerable scholarly evidence to indicate that a specific ethnic consciousness is not a new phenomenon. Raymond Wolfinger almost a decade ago demonstrated that in Eastern cities, ethnic voting patterns throughout the 1940's and 1950's persisted into the second and third generations.[2] Robert Dahl's classic work *Who Governs?* revealed that ethnicity had dominated the politics of New Haven for at least the four decades from 1920 to 1960, during which period Italians, Irish, Jews, Negroes, and Yankees struggled for the attention of radical and mainstream political parties.[3]

The political scientist Michael Parenti attempts to explain the persistence of specific political patterns for ethnic groups by suggesting that assimilation has not necessarily occurred when the ethnics have left their traditional urban ghettoes and been dispersed through suburbia.[4] Through the myriad of primary and secondary associations which it is the genuis of the American political system to foster, the various ethnic minorities seem to have erected a social sub-structure which has taken the place of the territorial unity once found in the cities:

> From birth in the sectarian hospital to childhood play-groups to cliques and fraternities in high school and college to the selection of a spouse, a church affiliation, social and service clubs, a vacation resort, and, as life nears completion, an old-age home and sectarian cemetery—the ethnic, if he so desires, may live within the confines of his sub-societal matrix—and many do.[5]

Thus over the last forty to sixty years the traditional political parties have paid considerable attention to the politics of ethnicity, and with good reason. If ethnicity is new or recently rediscovered by the intelligentsia, it is certainly not so for the politicians.[6] Similarly, as we will see shortly, the radical political parties have—at least in the past—been aware of the ethnic.

The impression current in the land, that ethnic consciousness is a conservative force and the specialty of mainstream politicians, is, of course, not without foundation. The renewal of the Nixonian mandate for another four years stems in part from Jewish ethnic identification with a strong pro-Israeli foreign policy and, more significantly, from the perception of white ethnics who constitute the electoral majority that Mr. Nixon was more likely to alleviate the employment and educational quotas that would favor certain minority ethnic groups

—Blacks, Puerto Ricans, Chicanos, Indians—through busing or affirmative action programs.

The response of Senator McGovern to the felt needs of the various ethnic groups was to deny that he was a "radical" opposed to ethnic solidarity, to assure the public that he stood four-square with the Jews on Israel, firmly for an Italian on the Supreme Court at the first convenient opening, and one thousand percent for federal aid to the ethnics' parochial schools.[7] In a word, the impact of majority white ethnic consciousness was to move even a man of such integrity as Senator McGovern to the right.

The 1972 presidential campaign merely provided a convenient showcase for the conservative political implications of ethnicity that have been building for several years and which persist and intensify even today. As the recent writings of Andrew Greeley and Michael Novak—and the reception given their writings—well indicate, the intellectual and political communities perceive the recent rise of white ethnicity to be ultimately opposed to the political interests of Blacks.[8]

In such a struggle, it is believed by many, the radical parties of the Left are at a disadvantage because their appeals should not be and cannot be based on ethnicity but must rely on transcendent ideological issues. The tradition of the Left as we perceive it today is, after all, that of an internationalist, cosmopolitan, class-oriented movement.[9] It is the parties of the Right which appeal to traditionalist, nationalist, racial, and ethnic interests in Europe, the Third World, and America.[10]

As a result of this tradition, the radical American political parties have suffered from disorientation and a self-imposed isolation from the focus of the political struggle over the last decade. After the white ethnic proletarians have been handed over from George Wallace's American Independent Party of 1968 to Richard Nixon's Republican Party of 1972, at a time when Black ethnics increasingly segregate themselves into their own political groupings, the traditional American radical political parties have been left without a constituency and have failed to bring their influence to bear effectively upon the social needs of contemporary American society.

It has not always been so.

Indeed, in a sense the political strategy of the radical parties in America has always been preeminently "ethnic." Frederick

Engels would introduce the name "Communists" to American readers in 1887 by attacking in a New York publication the fledgling Socialist Labor Party as "foreign to America, having until lately been made up almost exclusively of German immigrants, using their own language and, for the most part, little conversant with the common language of the country." Engels' prescription for the Socialist Labor Party was one which the various American ethnic groups were to hear time and time again:

> they will have to doff every remnant of their foreign garb. They will have to become out and out Americans. They cannot expect the Americans to come to them; they, the minority and the immigrants, must go to the Americans, who are the vast majority and the natives. And to do that, they must above all things learn English.[11]

There is a certain modernity to the advice.

The radical parties and Engels' own American Communist Party could not immediately follow his advice. In the beginning these radical socialist and communist political movements were as solicitous in courting white ethnic groups as the larger parties, and were even open to the Blacks.

The "radical" Knights of Labor, who flourished in the 1800's, included 60,000 Negroes among their membership of 700,000, drawn from all ethnic groupings in America.[12] The early history of most radical political parties in America was to follow a similar pattern. As Theodore Draper has well summarized it, "From the very outset, the American Socialist movement was peculiarly indebted to the immigrants for both its progress and its problems."[13] Engels, in 1893, lamented the difficulties encountered in America:

> Then, and more especially, immigration, which divides the workers into two groups: the native born and the foreigners, and the latter into 1) the Irish, 2) the Germans, 3) the many small groups, each of which understands only itself: Czechs, Poles, Italians, Scandinavians, etc. And then the Negroes. To form a single party out of these requires quite unusually powerful incentives.[14]

The failure of the socialist parties should not surprise us. In the Anglo-Saxon single-member district transmitted to America by Britain before the colonial tie was broken, there is an inevitable bias in favor of the political center in any electoral district and a gradual establishment of a party system consisting of the Government and the Opposition.[15] In such a system—geared towards aggregating a majority rather than representing proportionately every minority—the needs of those on the fringes of society are most likely to be ignored by the two major parties.

Historically, then, the third parties, the pariah parties of the Right and Left, have served as the first refuge of the new immigrants and—in the case of the Abolitionist movement[16]—of the Blacks. These minor parties have usually served as way stations, as a transmission belt which eventually led to the aggregation of this particular interest with the interests of many other groups into one of the two major political parties.[17]

Even while these small radical parties formally proclaimed ideological goals, their appeal was often in fact to those ethnics left out of the "American dream" or at least not yet a part of it. Gabriel Almond's study of 221 former American Communists, a majority of whom joined the party prior to 1935, indicated both the prevalence and the psychological links of this attraction:

> It would also appear that Communism may appeal to persons who feel rejected or are rejected by their environments. The image of the Communist militant is of a dignified, special person, dedicated, strong, confident of the future, a man who knows his objectives, does his duty without hesitation. These aspects of Communism have an obvious attraction for persons who carry within themselves feelings of being weak and unworthy as a consequence of early childhood experiences, as well as for persons who have been objectively rejected by their environments. The Negro, the Jew, the foreign-born, and the first-generation native-born, the unemployed, the native intellectual in a colonial country, may respond to their social situation by feeling rejected, unworthy, lacking in dignity and esteem. In this sense, any negatively discriminated status may contribute to susceptibility.[18]

Almond cites "racial and ethnic equality" as one of four main subcategories of "exoteric goals cited by the respondents as influencing their decision to join the party."[19]

Richard Burks, using a somewhat different methodology, has demonstrated that this relationship of radical political parties and membership in a less favored ethnic group existed beforehand in the East European countries from which many of the later immigrants came. During the inter-war period, allegiance to radical political parties at the polls or as an actual member is explained not so much by proletarian origin or status—as the formal goals of the party would imply—but more fundamentally by the "proclivity of certain ethnic groups for

the Communist cause." To a lesser extent, the same was true
for the socialist parties. Here in the motherland as in America,
men sought in radical politics an end to discrimination:

> We may erect almost as a principle the proposition that in Eastern Europe
> numerically weak ethnic groups produce above average numbers of Com-
> munists, providing these groups have a traditional tie to Russia. Other
> factors being equal, the weaker the ethnic group, the greater the proclivity.[20]

One may perhaps grasp a sense of the continuities and discon-
tinuities in the radical's espousal of ethnic consciousness during
the twentieth century by examining the relationship of American Blacks to radical political movements, specifically with
respect to the issue of separatism.

The creation in 1968 of a Black separatist Republic of New
Africa has led many to assume that Blacks are suddenly more
nationalist and ethnically conscious than in the past.[21] The
demand that this Republic be carved out of the five Southern
states of Louisiana, Mississippi, Alabama, Georgia, and South
Carolina, and that a Black propagandist, Robert Williams, then
resident in Peking, become the Republic's first president also
creates the illusion of an unprecedented radical threat.[22] But
the political history of our country shows that this is an enduring
theme, even to the point of the specific separatist strategies
being aided from foreign capitals.

By its nature, separatism is a radical political strategy. The
mainstream political parties could no more espouse Black
separatism than they could tolerate the South's secession.
However, for a political party in need of constituents and issues
on which to seize the attention of a mass audience, separatism
might well be viable.

As early as the 1830's the pioneer abolitionist Benjamin Lundy
actively proposed the radical solution of the American slave
problem through separation and colonization in Texas and
Haiti.[23] Ironically, at the height of its popularity in the late
1830's the colonization movement was to be denounced as a
conservative ploy seeking to remove from the scene free
Negroes and to perpetuate slavery.[24] By the 1840's Black
abolitionists were proposing a separate Black colony beyond
the Rocky Mountains.[25]

In the period from 1915 to 1917 Lenin wrote several essays
on America in which he maintained that "for the 'emancipated'

Negroes, the American South is a kind of prison where they are hemmed in, isolated and deprived of fresh air."[26] At the time, Lenin believed—mistakenly as it turned out—that the solution would be found in the Negro move to Northern cities.[27] Eventually, however, Lenin adopted the view that the American Negroes were an "oppressed nation," and he included them as one of the objects of Communist concern in his Preliminary Draft Theses on the National and Colonial Questions for the Second Congress of the Communist International in 1920.[8]

Just as Lenin goaded American Communists into recognizing the needs of the Negroes and the utility of the "oppressed nation" concept, after Lenin's death Moscow continued to supply guidance for the American Communist Party by suggesting the radical strategy of a separatist Black state. Although Theodore Draper in his recent *Rediscovery of Black Nationalism* correctly credits the 1928 Comintern Congress with adopting the doctrine of "the right of self-determination of the Negroes in the Black Belt" of the South, he also credits the American Communists with drawing up in 1936 a map of the Southern territory to be controlled by the Blacks.[29] Further research, however, shows that the map in James S. Allen's *The Negro Question in the United States* was almost certainly adapted from the extraordinary map in the 1933 Russian-language work of A. Amo on American Negro workers.[30]

After pursuing with a faint heart the Moscow-imposed separatist line for many years with little visible success, the American Communist Party in 1959 officially buried what it presumed was long dead and in the official Cominform journal rejected the idea of a Negro "nation" with a "common psychological make-up" distinguishing Blacks from other Americans.[31]

Ironically, the party had no sooner abandoned the ultraethnic position that had isolated it from the great majority of Blacks for forty years, than there was a significant shift on the part of Black popular opinion toward cultural distinctiveness and the concept that "Black is beautiful" developed. Peking and Robert Williams even formally established the long-sought Republic in the Black Belt with virtually the same boundaries set by Amo and Allen—though its future looked no more promising. Amid all the continuities, the Party had somehow lost out.

It is evident from what has already been said that ethnic consciousness and even so nationalist an aspiration as separatism are not inherently conservative political movements. As this brief historical survey has indicated, there is a rich tradition in America of radical espousal of the ethnic—and for good reasons.

Similarly the contemporary crisis in which the various ethnic groups struggle for the attention of the major political parties in order to retain territory, patronage, and educational and social benefits is not a new development in American political history.

What is perhaps new is the relative lack of effective advocacy of ethnic demands by the radical political parties of today. Perhaps, as Dahl suggests in *Who Governs?*, ethnic politics are a substitute for class politics, and the ideologically-oriented parties of the Left find it difficult to deal intelligently with ethnic issues.[32] The parties of the Left seem unable or unwilling to approach men as ethnics but prefer to employ class strategies focussed on economic issues. They see proletarians rather than Poles, Blacks, and Puerto Ricans.

Most of our ethnic groups started the climb to equality, however, by making use of the radical parties. It would be surprising, then, to find that these parties have no role for those ethnic groups, whether white or non-white, which still are not full participants in the American dream.

NOTES

1. William P. Randel, *The Ku Klux Klan, A Century of Infamy* (Philadelphia, 1965), details the history of the early Klan period from 1865 to 1877. The grievances of Southerners were not unlike the economic fears of today's suburban ethnics.

2. Raymond E. Wolfinger, "The Development and Persistence of Ethnic Voting," *American Political Science Review*, 59 (December 1965), pp. 896-908.

3. Robert A. Dahl, *Who Governs?* (New Haven, 1961), pp. 52-62.

4. Michael Parenti, "Ethnic Politics and the Persistence of Ethnic Identification," *American Political Science Review*, 61 (September 1967), pp. 717-726.

5. Ibid., p. 719. For detail, see for example Herbert J. Gans, *The Urban Villagers* (New York 1962) on the Italian community in Boston.

6. See Dahl, op. cit., pp. 32-62, on the political parties and the pursuit of the ethnic vote in New Haven; Parenti, op. cit., p. 717, n. 6; Robert C. Wood, *Suburbia, Its People and Their Politics* (Boston 1958), pp. 178 ff.

7. The significance of sectarian schools both in increasing ethnic consciousness and in facilitating a growing commitment among Catholics in religious conservatism and away from the Democratic party was first noted by Gerhard Lenski, *The Religious Factor* (Garden City, 1963, rev. ed.), pp. 268-270; and it was clearly demonstrated in the 1972 election.

8. Andrew Greeley, *Why Can't They Be Like Us?* (New York, 1971); Michael Novak, *The Rise of the Unmeltable Ethnics* (New York, 1971; Michael Novak and Silvano Tommusi, eds., *Who Speaks for Us?* (forthcoming). In the latter work, the chapter on "New Ethnic Politics vs. Old Ethnic Politics" gives a summary of critical reaction to Novak's first book. See also the spirited essay by Agnes Jackson in this issue of *Soundings*.

9. See, for example, the autobiographical statement of Louis Fischer with respect to Communism in Richard Crossman, ed., *The God That Failed* (New York, 1949), p. 202, and also the comments of Carl Landauer, a historian of socialism, in his *European Socialism* (Berkeley, 1959), vol. I, p. 808.

10. The comments of James Reston in the *New York Times* Nov. 1, 1972, p. 41, are typical.

11. Engels' comments are in his preface to the American edition of *The Condition of the Working Class in England* (New York, 1887), reprinted in Karl Marx and Frederick Engels, *On Britain*, 2nd ed. (Moscow, 1962), p. 13-14.

12. Louis Filler, *Crusaders for American Liberalism* (Yellow Springs, Ohio, 1964), p. 20; *On Britain*, p. 13, n. 1.

13. Theodore Draper, *The Roots of American Communism* (New York, 1957), p. 31.

14. Karl Marx and Frederick Engels, *Letters to Americans, 1848-1895* (New York, 1953), p. 258.

15. This analysis is most eloquently made in Ferdinand Hermens, *The Representative Republic* (Notre Dame, Indiana, 1958).

16. Louis Filler, *The Crusade Against Slavery, 1830-1860* (New York, 1963).

17. Gabriel Almond and G. Bingham Powell, Jr., *Comparative Politics: A Developmental Approach* (Boston, 1966), pp. 98 ff.

18. Gabriel Almond, *The Appeals of Communism* (Princeton, N.J., 1954), pp. 279-282.

19. Ibid., p. 140.

20. Richard V. Burks, *The Dynamics of Communism in Eastern Europe* (Princeton, N.J., 1961), p. 188; see also, pp. 73-87, 187-9, 163-170.

21. *New York Times*, April 1, 1968, p. 22.

22. Ibid., Sept. 21, 1968, p. 14; July 13, 1972, p. 23.

23. Louis Filler, *Crusade*, op. cit., p. 26.

24. Louis Filler, *Slavery in the United States of America*, (New York, 1972), p. 104.

25. *Common Objections to Going to Liberia Answered* (n.p., n.d.), in Filler, *Slavery*, p. 105.

26. Vladimir I. Lenin, *Collected Works*, 2nd Engl. ed. (Moscow, 1960), vol. 22, p. 27.

27. Ibid., vol. 20, p. 30, and vol. 39, p. 455.

28. See Lenins's January 1917 essay, "Statistics and Sociology," in Ibid, vol. 23, pp. 275-6 and vol. 31, p. 148.

29. Theodore Draper, *The Rediscovery of Black Nationalism* (New York, 1970), pp.63-64.

30. James S. Allen, *The Negro Question in the United States* (New York, 1936), p. 17, and see pp. 177-181; A. Amo, *Negrityakskiye rabochiye v Soedinyennikh Shtatakh* [*Negro Workers in the United States*] (Moscow, 1933), p. 12.

31. James Jackson, "Some Aspects of the Negro Question in the United States," *World Marxist Review*, vol. 2, no. 7, pp. 16-24.

32. Dahl, op. cit., p. 59.

ETHNIC REVIVALISM, BLUE-COLLARITES, AND BUNKER'S LAST STAND

ARTHUR B. SHOSTAK

When we get to the place in the development of our society where the tools of abundance can take care of the material needs of the outer man with less and less human effort, the real emphasis then has to be shifted to enabling the inner man to grow. In other words, we've got to develop new appetites, new interest in non-material things . . .

Walter Reuther, 1960

The majority of men in advanced industrial societies are often confused, unhappy, and conscious of their lack of power; they are also often hopeful, critical, and able to grasp immediate possibilities of happiness and freedom.

Alasdair MacIntyre, "On Marcuse," *New York Review of Books*, October 23, 1969, p. 38.

THERE ARE TIMES when I can almost hear some twentieth-century equivalent of Mr. Dooley, Finley Peter Dunne's sagacious bartender, leaning forward over his highly polished bartop to softly ask in a magical Irish lilt, "My boy, privately now and only between us, how really real is this so-called Ethnic Revival? Why the big hoorah at *this* time? And why the blarney about its medicinal properties? Will grown men never tire of the outgrown playthings of their youth?" Puzzled in like fashion I want to explore our joint concern below, Hennessey's, Dooley's, and mine, and push further to suggest an alternative interpretation of and prescription for the social discontents that

Born into an Italian working-class neighborhood, Mr. Shostak has published widely on working-class issues, including his *Blue-Collar Life* (1968) and his forthcoming *The Rich and the Poor*. He is an Associate Professor in the Department of Social Sciences at Drexel University in Philadelphia.

some students of ethnicity are now linking to the Great Ethnic Awakening, whatever that is.

I

When visiting a typical blue-collar enclave in the city nowadays I am often struck by the commonplace use there of colorful ethnic ensigns (car decals in nationality colors, bumper stickers, or lapel buttons—"Irish Power," "Slovak Power," etc.). Similarly, when reflecting in my course in "Race and Ethnic Relations" on the longstanding activist role of B'nai Brith's Anti-Defamation League I am quickly drawn along by eager white ethnic students to a tentative appraisal of the bold new role of the ill-starred Italian-American Anti-Defamation League and its enormous (if haunted) Columbus Day rallies. When I combine all these signs of new ethnic assertiveness and competency with the media spotlight on it all (in Sunday supplement features as well as TV situation comedies) I am momentarily swayed in favor of the seemingly self-evident assertion that we are experiencing an Ethnic Revival of considerable proportions, far-reaching significance, and possibly even of lasting impact.

Perhaps. But with my bartender friend I am really not sure. Indeed, I have serious reservations about all of this—the reality of the Revival, the appropriateness of such a Revival for what really ails a sector of the white ethnic population (the blue-collarites), and the factual clarity and real charity of those cultural interpreters like myself who are endlessly in and out of some alleged revival or another.

Note that my narrow academic focus (and personal history) make appropriate a strict concern with only a sub-sample of the larger white ethnic sample out of the entire universe of contemporary Americans. Having grown up with Jewish shopkeeper parents in an Italian "urban village" section of Brooklyn, New York, I have not surprisingly made something of an academic career of trying to make sense of it all: my old neighborhood, public schooling, gentile friends, occasional beatings, lost innocence, personal quest, and the commonplace rest. Two books and a dozen articles later I pursue it still, in this particular essay with a special focus on younger blue-collarites (under 35) of increasingly higher educational attainment, religious disaffection, political volatility, and suburban orientation (if urban now, suburban soon!).

II

Four years ago, in a monograph exploring the life-styles of just such a dynamic young adult and his more numerous conservative and older associates in blue-collar ranks, I urged that the new attention be paid to the persistence of ethnicity in the life style of all blue-collarites.* Now, I find myself perplexed by just that development. For what I see about me in the way of attention being paid combines so much bombast, so little refinement, and possibly so misguided a prescription for life as to leave me seriously concerned lest blue-collar white ethnics take our flurry of academic interest at all seriously.

Bombast ingloriously substitutes for empirical evidence of the existence of the very Ethnic Revival itself. It would seem fair to expect certain kinds of hard data from Revival enthusiasts (or denigrators) beyond the insistence, "Well, everyone just knows it!"

For example, has anyone thought to investigate longitudinal changes in the number and audience of our foreign-language radio shows, newspapers, and magazines? After adjusting data here for our record-setting immigrations of recent years (373,000 in 1970 alone, the second highest number since 1924), this material on followership could be combined with that on recent changes in the dues-paying rolls of ethnic organizations to reveal much about the hard substance really inside the Revival ballyhoo. Similarly, attention might profitably be paid to changes occuring over time in the intermarriage rates among our no longer insular nationalities and across the "border" that separates hyphenated Americans from British-Americans (as Michael Novak suggests we re-christen the WASPs). Finally, research might extend beyond tried-and-true indices (such as crowd attendance at ethnic holiday parades and court records of applications for the Americanization of Old Country names) to some more venturesome and potentially revealing new components of the scene, e.g., the stress apparently no longer placed on ethnicity in parochial schools by modern lay teachers, or the lack of stress on ethnicity by parents who shop for private

---

*Shostak, Arthur B., *Blue-collar Life* (New York, 1968). I wrote then, and contend anew in this essay, that "too much at present has too many members of the working class making too little of their lives . . . America's working class is one that fears to dare, figures small angles incompetently, and makes the least-best of its life-enhancing possibilities" (p. 291).

schooling or who favor enactment of the Voucher Plan for subsidized private schooling for all.

Without such data we are sorely handicapped. And, unless properly collected, even snippets of data that do become available do not always carry us much further ahead. Typical is the problem posed by large-scale travel statistics that verify an impressive amount of ethnic American travel back to the Auld Sod. Not only is the subject clouded by the recent date at which detente has made much of this travel tenable (as to Eastern European nations); the data grievously fail to separate travelers by social class or age. If disproportionately few ethnics who are both under 45 years of age and are of blue-collar status are flying "home" to "see the family tree" (as a British Airlines ad beckons) the travel surge might be considered more an index of desperation than of confirmation, that is to say, more a return to fading memories by sentimental and well-heeled oldsters than a proud claiming of new roots by tradition-hungry and meaning-seeking younger working-class ethnics.

Is there an Ethnic Revival then, or isn't there? Plainly, we just do not know. And, given the dust cloud raised by politicians of every persuasion in lusty quest of this or that real or imagined ethnic bloc vote, 1973 may be an especially inauspicious year to try to find out. This much *is* clear: Ethnic pride ensigns, leagues, rallies, and media celebrity status do not alone an Ethnic Revival make.

III

Equally clear, if no less perplexing, is the remarkable revival of interest in ethnicity among men of letters. Why? Two explanations stand out. First, like the Blacks before them in the 1960's, the white ethnics have fairly forced themselves upon the consciousness (and conscience) of the intellectual community in recent years. And second, men of ideas—many of them—are looking full circle back to their personal origins or to their romanticized notions of ethnic origins for new clues to living the Good Life in a sanitized Sears, Roebuck/Disneyland world too blah for their still robust appetites.

There is first, then, the issue of the clamor raised in blue-collar neighborhoods by white ethnics who are raucously demanding—everything! Not just "law and order," which the mocking and derogatory media over-stress, but also tax reductions, a return to educational fundamentals, enlargement of the consumer advocacy role of government, and equity with people of color in the distribution of scarce (and inadequate) social welfare expenditures. "You all have been getting yours for long enough," the battlecry goes; "now we want ours!"

First given clear expression in the Wallace campaign of 1968, this motif assaults the popular intellectual rendering of an Affluent Society inside which the vast majority of "end-of-ideology" manual workers are credit-card happy and Big Labor secure. But even as it took the Triple Deaths (Kennedy, King, Kennedy) to compel a far more honest understanding of the harshness and brutishness common in life, so also has it taken the brutal murders of the Yablonskis, the savage crippling of Joe Colombo, and the "self-destruct-on-Skag" habit of blue-collar veterans of Vietnam to shake the false euphoria and complacency from the intellectual view of blue-collar life.[1]

Why the revival, then, of egghead interest in manual workers? Because the piercing outcry of blue-collar discontent, and the enormous "dues" of neglect in the form of decay and terror in the cities, which egghead and worker uneasily share, have forced men of letters to take note. A shopworn scenario, you think, one with a strong ring of familiarity? Of course, since in most important ways it hews close to the more inclusive pacesetting black-white scenario of the last fifteen years.

Save in this one critical difference: Many well-degreed Caucasian interpreters of white ethnicity, themselves often among the first of their Old Country bloc to attain intellectual distinction (by British-American standards) take now to press to ruminate publicly about the meaning of it all, and most especially about the ethnic ethos they plaintively wish to somehow preserve in their own homogenizing suburbias. Mixing unequal parts of nostalgia (the "white lie" variety), recrimination (the British-Americans as heavies), and romance (Novak's New Ethnic Consciousness, a sublime achievement in Maslow-like universal self-actualization), the white commentators "go home" as they never could before, in their strained and once-removed commentary on Black realities.

They posit new interpretations of failure:

The Irish in New York represent a way of life that never was Irish. The Irish always were poor and they measured value by other than material things. They sang and told stories and used words for entertainment. Their descendants in New York can't wait to get into the banking business.[2]

And they posit new models of success, even if they are of a strained and desperate variety: Little Italy plays host weekends to "Saturday's Italians," or those prospering, overweight sons of leaner immigrant fathers who drive in now from suburbia on weekends to replenish their ever-diminishing ethnic supplies:

> They return, after all, not only for the bread, tiny bitter onions, bushels of snails, live eels and dried cod, but also to enjoy a weekend heritage that their education, blond wives, and the English language have begun to deny them . . . it is only with a trunk filled with Italian market produce that a Saturday Italian can face six days in the suburbs.[3]

Above all, however, they make plain how much anguish, confusion, and "future shock" we share across our class and ethnic and racial chasms—and, in this very way, ironically undermine the erstwhile point of the alleged Ethnic Revival they think they celebrate.

IV

For along with the bombast-in-place-of-evidence issue touched on earlier, there is a related critical matter, the costly lack of refinement, or calibration, that so taxes the entire subject. Viewed through the wire-rimmed spectacles of the visiting "made good" ex-local boy, the blue-collarite's problems as a white ethnic come finally to resemble far too closely the problems one can readily expect of marginal (first-generation) intellectuals themselves: "Archie's" aches get lost in the eagerness of the writers to air their own *Angst*, attributing it all to "Archie." The writer longs to return to an ethos that is more Archie's defeat than his deliverance, however differently it be viewed from outside.

Blue-collar women, for example, bitterly denounce their homey prototype "Edith Bunker" when I ask about this popular TV heroine in my research. They especially disown her Old Country passivity, naiveté, and doltishness. Working outside their homes and ethnic neighborhoods, as many do, these free-wheeling women are often aggressive, sophisticated, and mentally adroit. Long accustomed, as in the case of the culturally assimilated movie wife of *Joe*, to manipulating the men folk (of all ages), modern blue-collar women more often resemble (and seem to identify with) Gloria than Edith in the Bunker household.

Similarly, young blue-collarites of both sexes find Archie at times a bit hard to recognize, since many either have long since helped direct their fathers away from the Old Country mold or have grudgingly moved far away from the "lost cause" of an obsolete Old Man, and it is just this notion of chronic tension, special effort, and ultimate resolution that underlies my particular perspective on what it is that *is* bothering Bunker—and what we might all help do about it.

I see Archie hurting not so much from the loss of ethnicity as from a lingering attachment to it! In many costly ways he uses his Old World ethnicity as a second-rate shield against a host of new personal and intimate demands put on him by the hardest audience of all to deny, his own family members.

Preoccupied with the white ethnic's 8 A.M. to 5 P.M. problems (the assembly-line speedup, the dead-end job ladder, the threat of technological displacement) we have paid grossly inadequate attention to the related discontents of his 5 P.M. to 8 A.M. existence. Or, narrowly sensitive to his after-work role as citizen, voter, and ethnic, we have paid far too little attention to him in his roles as husband, lover, father and son. Yet it is exactly here, in a "role-crunch" that dwarfs anything the script-writers for the Bunkers seem equal to, that white ethnics may especially hurt—and find yesterday's ethnicity-as-remedy irrelevant.

V

Historically the personal role expectations of manual workers were dominated, almost regardless of ethnicity, by a *machismo* model of rugged containment (as husbands), virile braggadocio (as lovers), authoritarian rule (as fathers), and proper role-distance (as sons). As a husband the blue-collar male expected to "keep 'em in their place." As a lover he would "get all he could." As a father he would damn well "teach them their place." And in his own mature years as a middle-aged son he would give the old 'uns only what he must to keep up appearances in the extended family and the old neighborhood.

From one generation to another, role expectations mellowed only slightly, by and large as a correlate of the inter-generational weakening of a rigid ethnic strait jacket (male supremacy, "good woman"/"bad woman" framework, and the rest). In most cases blue-collar men lived so as to expect little friendship in marriage, little ecstasy in (marital) sex relations, little intimacy in fatherhood, and little affect in arms-length dealings with the "old man." Instead they clung unhappily to a gruff image of themselves as "real men"—or hard, undemonstrative "sons of bitches."

Now, what seems to have been happening in the last twenty-five years is the collapse of the underlying psycho-social "contract" that helped hold this all together. Blue-collar women, heady with their new-found freedom from conception fears and challenged by the gossip of still-better-lives-yet that they pick up at work or from the TV, impose a host of new role expectations upon their husbands or lovers. Blue-collar children, coming home daily from schools more cosmopolitan than ever before, eager recruits themselves to the best-heeled teen culture of all times, and TV addicts par excellence, ask more of the father than ever before in white ethnic households. And blue-collar seniors, heavily burdened with financial debt and the costs of their psychic unreadiness for forced retirement, demand of their adult sons a degree of financial and emotional aid unprecedented in blue-collar affairs.

Where once the blue-collar male was free to be a self-centered, self-gratifying Marlboro Country cowboy, he is now expected to aspire in drastically other directions. A new role-set asks him to strive for frank and genial affability with most, deep-coursing personal intimacy with some, and erotic artfulness with a very select few. His family (if not his church leaders, ethnic spokesmen, or academic interpreters!) expect, indeed demand that they all live now as other than muffled human beings, disappointed in life and in one another. They set their faces firmly against the Old World anxieties and divisions that would tax them so, and struggle to replace dogma and taboo with the excitement of a life engagingly explored.[4]

Not all, by any means, but many. And of these, large numbers are under 35 years of age. Therein lies still another key point with which I will draw to a close this round-about espousal of a substitute analysis for that of the Great Ethnic Awakening.

VI

None of this is meant to gloss over significant differences inside the category of blue-collar ethnics. Much of the "role crunch" is escaped by those over 50, directly experienced by those between 35 and 50, stoutly resisted by those between 20 and 35, and quizzically observed by those between 15 and 20. Inside these age brackets a further breakdown separates foreign-born (less vulnerable) from third-generation native-born (most vulnerable), immobile (less vulnerable) from upwardly mobile (more vulnerable), and Immigrant Church-oriented (less vulnerable) from Mainstream Catholic (more vulnerable, given the Protestant-like alterations in modern Catholic attitudes and practices). When fractionated in this fashion the rich diversity can be seen in what is artificially perceived as a bloc, and its internal dynamism is more readily grasped.

This dynamism helps explain the otherwise contradictory existence, side by side, of both traditions of interest in this essay, or the worker's lingering romance with Old World ethnicity and his newer flirtation with his own version of New World modernism. To be sure, the largest number of blue-collarites at this time hew closer to the ethnic mold than to modernistic derring-do. And this is likely to remain true through the late 1980's But given the disproportionately large bloc of youngsters coming along (12 is the largest age group in our population) this situation may be already changing, with the working class having possibly generated its own revolutionary cultural vanguard from within!

At present for example, many "vanguard" blue-collarites appear to be closing the class rifts to join comparable middle-class rebels in redoing their own native Church. The so-called underground Catholic Church draws them with the hope that its person-centeredness, its humanism, its erotic, sensual possibilities, and, above all, its bold incorporation of psyche-expanding encounter techniques will help them grow as their fathers cannot (or dare not?). Others look to media innovations, both sexes tuning in avidly to new radio talk shows astonishing

---

*An exceptionally fine essay on such solid (and stolid) blue-collarites, "tragic victims requiring more attention and social concern than they have received thus far," is available in "Working-Class Youth: Alienation without an Image," by William Simon and John H. Gagnon, in *The White Majority*, edited by Louise Kapp Howe (New York, 1970), pp. 45-60.

in their sex relations candor, and to psychoanalytic explorations of real-life dilemmas ("The Family Game," etc.). Many also turn regularly to ever-bolder media columnists (Dr. Reuben, Marya Mannes, Dr. Hippocrates, etc.) in the underground as well as the conventional press, and take instruction in modernity from the glossy likes of *Playboy* and *Cosmopolitan* while their parents stick to *True* and *True Confessions*, *Argosy* and *Photoplay*, *True Detective* and *TV/Radio Mirror*.

Many find ethnicity inimicable to a host of role options that seem to require freedom from taboos, Old Country strictures, and xenophobic prejudice. Pace-setters among them dare to countenance guiltless pre-marital relations, casual trial marriages, unapologetic single parenthood, readily secured abortions, considerable sexual experimentation, easy no-fault divorce, single adult adoptions, and other deep-running challenges to conventional morality. Some of their leisure practices extend far beyond the borders of what "our people" have always (and only) enjoyed, and a full range of public behaviors (opting for circumcision of all male infants, choosing cremation over burial, etc.) rattle the bars of the ethnic "jailhouse." Indeed, the more astute among them decline to blame themselves alone for the "role-crunch" they are challenged by and insightfully find sources of responsibility as well in the larger social order. Accordingly, unlike their staid ethnic counterparts many of these blue-collar moderns take seriously the case being made today for nationalized health care (which would include subsidized counseling and psychiatry), nationwide day care (which would include professional parent education), a guaranteed annual wage, earlier retirement, sabbatical leave, and the like, tradition-shattering though they may be.

Because an ethnic/modern split of such proportions has substantial political and public policy ramifications, it will undoubtedly strain affinities among blue-collarites for decades to come. But the handwriting is already on the wall. And while some ethnic purists see it only as "Clockwork Orange" graffiti, other translators such as myself read a very different message into it: Wary of the eviscerating perils of naive assimilation ("Into what?" sarcastically ask ethnic spokesmen as otherwise disparate as Eldridge Cleaver, Michael Novak, Rabbi Cahane, and Elijah Muhammad), America's blue-collarites will probably long continue to use ethnicity in a fashion uniquely their own. Many rely on an ethnic vote to control their labor union locals and insure at least some direct representation in city council chambers. Many use their informal ethnic studies (traditions, culture, philosophy) as a bulwark against the psychic toll of Toffler's "future shock," even as some lean on it also for a defense against the modernity of their own young. And large numbers are presently wringing every last ounce of aid from it as they struggle with the challenge of an extraordinary "role-crunch," one that superficially appears to force a choice between the Scylla of retrograde ethnicity and the Charybdis of Mass Culture assimilation.

To their considerable credit a variety of blue-collarites, old and young alike, already seem to grasp with keen insight the hazard of a *false* choice here. For some time now opinion-shapers among them have fought to impose their *own* design on the entire situation, a design which has them seek the best of both options, the most that can be had from *both* ethnicity and mass culture. Blue-collarites of this persuasion distinguish the square from the plastic:

> Squareness implies a strong dose of personal and cultural scruple; plasticity is the attempt to be fashionable without paying the price. Going to church out of religious conviction, however understood (or misunderstood), may be square; going to church for social reasons is plastic. "God Bless America" and "Semper Fidelis" are square; Lester Lanin playing the Beatles is plastic. Busby Berkeley musicals are square; *The Sound of Music* is plastic. Billy Sunday was square; Billy Graham is plastic. . . .[5]

The blue-collar amalgam of Old Country ethnicity and New World modernity I have reference to is decidedly square. Indeed, it seems increasingly unique to that class, as the rest of the culture gravitates either toward the dead-end ethnic revival of the non-white minorities or the gray assimilationism of the majority mainstreamers. While many politicians, sociologists, and journalists are crudely unable to distinguish the square from the plastic, and mistakenly insist our choice is only between Ethnicity (good) and Modernity (bad), blue-collarites, possibly enough to make a profound difference, see it—and live it—otherwise.

This is *not* to romanticize their life-style proclivities, however attractive their rejection of the *ersatz* quality of the plastic life that cheapens or deadens everything it touches. Their squareness has its full share of blind spots and hazards for its holders and for us all, though these shortcomings pale alongside the comparable pitfalls of the false dichotomy commonly imagined by outside commentators. What especially attracts about blue-collar squareness, however, is its class-based origins (fed by ethnic "springs"), its class-linked integrity, and its class-grounded openness to political popularism.[6]

Some flavor of what I am driving at, of what I make of the class-inspired "graffiti" on the wall, might be better conveyed here from the "vanguard" example of Mrs. Bette Lowrey, a 47-year-old suburban wife of a machinist, who was identified in 1970 by the media as meeting the expert's profile of the typical voter:

> But in the flesh she also turned out to be more decent than the political projections, more complex than the statistics, and more informed than Agnew and his speechwriters took her to be. "I wish," she said, "that people would do more listening. All these kids wouldn't be rioting if they didn't have good reasons. Sometimes it takes rioting and dissent to bring change." Mrs. Lowrey, as it turned out, had a twenty-one-year-old son with long hair.[7]

Blue-collar "squares" of this ilk promote their own version of the mainstream, one that would have irreverence long persist in America, and one that helps keep alive the hope that diverse constituencies can still be rallied against the impersonal, the systematic, and perhaps even the plastic.[8]

Note that their irreverence extends to their own ethnicity, and that such blue-collarites decline to make a new false idol out of the accident of their ethnic origins. Typical is the rejection experienced here by a Polish American millionaire deeply committed to promoting the so-called Ethnic Revival:

> above all, they wish they were solvent. They look at a millionaire like Piszek, realize that he has already spent a quarter of a million dollars on a handsomely bound Golden Book of Knowledge about Poland, and wonder why in hell he isn't throwing some of that cash their way if he has so damned much to waste. The Poles . . . feel that they can get all the culture they need at the parish hall or at CYO folk dances. What they want is money up front. They'd gladly call Ed Piszek "super-Pole" if he could push the Puerto Ricans out of [their neighborhood], help them pay the loan companies on time, and keep the streets clean.[9]

Hardly an inspiring agenda, and exactly the sort of thing likely to get the *New York Times* down on them. But in its unabashed honesty about priorities and its indulgent disdain for plastic airs, this Polish "Middle American" squareness is its own justification—and a striking qualification of the premature announcement of a Great Ethnic Awakening.

What *is* awakening in certain blue-collar quarters is a new interest in old populist issues, along with a small and novel "vanguard" concern with cultural reforms. The absence of George Wallace from the 1972 Presidential campaign, for example, was sorely missed by many blue-collarites (and millions of others as well). For alongside his convoluted racism there was an engaging populist streak as he played to people increasingly impatient with the pieties and equivocations of established mainstream rhetoric. Wallace dared to run against banks and utilities, foundations and distant planners, bosses and ivory-tower theorists. Many of his younger supporters were, and could again be, blue-collar workers with no special loyalty to the old Democratic Party or to the professional labor leaders who purport to represent them.

Instead, this large and volatile section of the white working-class shops about now for some new locus for its loyalites—and its dreams. Its untutored and incoherent populism crops out in diverse and revealing ways—in the Lordstown revolt of the young workers; the move for school control by blue-collar neighborhood residents; their failure to seriously press for an end to the so-called pornography explosion; the remarkably fast adoption by Catholics of oral contraceptives; and the openness to a fiery kind of female political spokeswoman previously laughed out of ethnic politics (e.g., Baltimore's Barbara Mikulski and Boston's Louise Day Hicks).

Often vulgar and schizophrenic, sometimes contradictory and chaotic, and not infrequently compassionate, this new blue-collar culture can still stumble and finally prove to be little more than an interim experience on the way to what Dwight Macdonald condemns as "the agreeable ooze of the Midcult swamp." But then again, it might not. For, disdainful of both Old Country ethnicity *and* Mainstream plasticity, the bulk of manual workers sustain a time-honored attachment to their square blue-collar ethos even as they uneasily allow breathing space to the few exotic cultural revisionists or young "vanguard" moderns in their midst.

Pure ethnicity of the variety called for by enthusiasts of the Awakening leaves most of these self-conscious blue-collarites cold, as they suspect it is too readily turned to "plastic," know it for its divisive peril, and reject its ability to let social class issues go into hiding. Because of its availability for turning co-workers against each other, reinvigorated ethnicity comes in second best to the promotion of a "square" class culture—and a begrudging tolerance for the moddish ways of the select young.

And this, rather than a costly re-direction of blue-collar culture, could continue to characterize the gropings of that social class for many years to come, in a fashion instructive and enlarging for us all—provided we allow for the pluralism herein entailed and relax our missionary zeal for ethnic (though not for class-populist) renewal.[10]

VII

Is there really an Ethnic Revival? Why do some salute it even as others still call for it? How much more can we learn of the worker's plight by focusing instead on role and class turbulence? Do the choices of renewed ethnicity or eviscerating assimilationism really exhaust the working-class options, or is there possibly a third, overlooked possibility in an eclectic amalgam of three related traditions—vanguard youthful modernity, square (as contrasted with plastic) culture, and updated populism? And how much of a disservice might we possibly perform in our momentary academic advocacy of an Ethnic Awakening, except as we remain open at the same time to alternative analyses and prescriptions? If it is pluralism we intend to promote, it should begin with our academics, especially if we are to play a constructive part ourselves in ongoing blue-collar developments that are possibly a good deal more vital and humanizing than our current ethnic preoccupations.

NOTES

1. Brilliant in this connection is "Betrayed American Workers," by Richard Sennett and Jonathan Cobb, in *The New York Review of Books* (October 5, 1972), pp. 31-33.
2. Jimmy Breslin, "The True Irish Export," *New York World Journal Tribune* (March 12, 1967), pp. 6-7; see also Joe Flaherty, "The Men of Local 1268, God Bless Them All, the Last of a Bad Breed," *New York* (Sept. 12, 1972), pp. 56-58.
3. Nicholas Pileggi, "Saturday Italians," *New York World Journal Tribune* (January 15, 1967), pp. 12, 14.

4. I draw here from a longer essay of mine, "Middle-Aged Working Class Americans at Home: Changing Expectations of Manhood," *Cornell Occupational Mental Health* (Fall 1972), pp. 2-7. See also Robert Coles, *The Middle Americans* (Boston, 1971).

5. Peter Schrag, *The Decline of the WASP* (New York, 1971), p. 193 *passim.*

6. For my own strongest public exploration of this thesis, see "Blue-Collar Prospects—Grey, White, or Green Collar?" in *IRRA Proceedings, 1972* (Madison, Wisconsin, 1972); also New Working Class?" *New Politics* (Fall 1972), pp. 29-43.

7. Schrag, *op. cit.*, p. 186. See also Robert E. Lane and Michael Lerner, "Why Hard-Hats Hate Hairs," *Psychology Today* (November 1970), pp. 45-49.

8. Helpful in this connection is Andrew M. Greeley, "New Ethnicity and Blue Collars," *Dissent* (Winter 1972), pp. 270-77. See also Frank Riessman, "The Backward Vanguard,' *Society* (November/December, 1972), pp. 104-6.

9. Mike Mallowe, "What's Polish, Has Two Legs and Finally Has Gotten Its Dander Up?" *Philadelphia Magazine* (November 1972), p. 113.

10. Invaluable for guidance here is *Beyond Black or White: An Alternative America*, edited by Vernon J. Dixon and Badi Foster (Boston, 1971).

"GYPSIES":

People with a Hidden History

GLEN W. DAVIDSON

T HEY CALL THEMSELVES the *Rom*, though they use the moni-
kers imposed on them by others to their own advantage.
Rom, in their language, means "man." Their term for us
is *gadje*, which means "foreigners" or "strange ones." In the
days of the frontier, the *Rom* were called "tinkers" and were
prohibited entrance into most taverns and road houses, not to
speak of more reputable institutions.

Despised as much for their supposed origin as for their vocations and nomadic tendencies, they were early identified as
"Egyptians" or "Gypsies." And the slang abbreviation "gyp"
has become our preferred word for swindle, fraud, and cheat.
At times their presence is flamboyantly obvious and they gener-
ate the most bizarre fantasies in the *gadje*'s imagination. But
most of the time they are invisible, even though their race is
represented in almost every major city of the continent.

Until 1972, when the United States Supreme Court struck
down the loose use of the term "vagrant," forty-one states of
the union implicitly, and Delaware explicitly, made their race
synonymous with vagrancy and prohibited their presence. Vagrancy laws, particularly as interpreted and applied at the municipal and county levels of government, were used to harrass the
Rom, but law didn't prevent them from moving where whim
directed.

There is very little written about the *Rom*, and almost all
of it has been written by *gadje*. There are those sensitive reports

Mr. Davidson is Associate Professor of Culture and Medicine, Southern
Illinois University School of Medicine, Springfield. Part of his study of the
Rom was supported by the University of Iowa Graduate Faculty and The
Newberry Library.

by writers who have respected and lived with them.[1] But more
prevalent are the academic works which seek to objectify and
quantify them in history. As a record about man such history
is interesting and permits us to see relationships not otherwise
in view. But have we yet answered the question of who the
Rom are?

When one looks at many of the studies of ethnic groups
in North America, particularly those examinations made by
social scientists, a standard selection of data seems to be used
to answer the question of identity—"Who are they?" The data
are origin—"Where did they come from?"; vocation—"What
do they do?"; and quantity—"How many of them are there?"
All too often the answers tell us little but allow us to stereotype
with all the authority prejudice permits.

On the basis of the work of German philologists it is widely
assumed among scholars today that the *Rom* originated in India.
Romany, their language, is similar to Sanskrit. Linguists, however, can also trace and date many "loan words" apparently
picked up along assumed routes of migration through Asia
Minor and Eastern Europe.

Nomadic tribes believed to be Gypsies are mentioned in European records as early as the thirteenth century A.D. By 1370
they appeared in the records of Walachia, 1407 in Germany,
1419 in France, 1422 in Italy, 1430 in England, 1500 in Russia,
and 1512 in Sweden. Almost all of the records raise the question
about the origin of these unsettling wanderers.

The earliest record of the Gypsies in the British American
colonies seems to have been written by a judge in Henrico
County, Virginia, in 1695, though we know that Scottish Gypsies
were transported to the plantations during most of the second
half of the seventeenth century.[2] There is evidence that Gypsies
were in French Louisiana, among the German settlers of Penn-
sylvania, and with the Dutch in New Amsterdam. But, according to the Pinkerton Agency archives, sizeable immigration of
Gypsies did not occur until the 1840's, when the events leading
up to the Rural Police Act passed by the British Parliament
made nomadic life unbearable. But whatever the *Rom*'s true
origin, India, or Egypt, or land unknown, they are not European
and have thereby always been greeted with overt suspicion in
North America.

But if the *Rom* did originate in India, where did they come from before then? Were they among pariah castes? What does that tell us about them now? The problem raised by the *Rom* is that they themselves do not base their identity on space or time, except to speak of where they were "yesterday." Few have been permitted to settle and thereby take on a "land" identity. Time is spoken of in terms of family relationships, not reigns of kings. The question of identity is not alone answered by objectifying and quantifying the *Rom* in place and time. There is precious little evidence to objectify. The history of the *Rom* is hidden in their symbols and rituals.

Allan Pinkerton estimated in 1878 that "in the United States alone they now number fully one hundred thousand souls," many of whom entered the United States illegally.[3] Later writers have "guesstimated" that today there are as many as a million *Rom* in North America and five million in the world. These guessers have absolutely nothing upon which to base their figures except their own imaginations. No census has ever been made of the Gypsies on this continent, and the *Rom*'s attempt to keep hidden would make any census suspect. There is precious little evidence to quantify. Their numbers are hidden even to themselves.

The thesis of this essay is that the *Rom* illustrate the need to look both for the "objective" history of a people and its "subjective" history—the history of "meaning" as understood within the people's own frames of reference. And that requires that when we look at the question of identity we include the data of destiny—"Where are they going?"

I have been searching for the *Rom*'s data of destiny for three years. From my childhood I remember their annual appearance at our ranch in Idaho. But then I feared and avoided them. Through friendship with a priest who has directed much of his ministry toward meeting the needs of the *Rom* in Chicago, I found entrance into their homes and lives. In Quebec, New York, Iowa, Illinois, and Idaho I have been attempting to understand the identity of the *Rom* through their own symbols and rituals. This essay is the first attempt.

The story I relate centers around one man, though it could be told of numerous other Gypsies. Because of the *Rom*'s need to protect themselves they adapt to their context. Therefore my interpretations should be understood as descriptive only of the *Rom* I know. One learns quickly that the ways of the

Rom and their identity characteristics cannot be readily generalized in the *gadje*'s frames of reference.

A Gypsy male was admitted to a university hospital with advanced cancer of the lungs. He was approximately 45 years of age, the father of five children, and "variously employed." Despite the fact that a large number of Gypsies soon gathered in the hospital lobby to express concern about him, thereby making the patient's presence an irregular occurrence in the hospital's routine, the case history recorded at the time read:

> Puerto Rican male, shows contempt for his condition, persists in smoking, and frequently violates care plan. Roman Catholic. On welfare. Easily excited and very nervous. Recommend no visitors.

The social worker who wrote the case history of the patient assumed that such "histories" have basic importance for both knowing how to interpret the patient's present condition and how to better prepare the patient's hospital care plan. She gave significance to race, sex, religion, and economic status—though she recorded the wrong race and religion. Knowing this, she thought, the health care team could better understand the ways the patient expressed himself and better predict the ways the patient could be expected to cope with his illness and hospitalization. Instead, the report, since it was interpreted as containing "objective" data, was used by the health care staff to justify their prejudiced opinions about him. Standardized procedures permit efficient hospital operations and quality control, but when they are imposed thoughtlessly on a patient they may violate his definition of health and his sense of appropriate behavior. This would negate the goal of health care, which is to meet the patient's basic needs.

The patient was called Stephen Jones—not his "real" name, though it was one of several he used with his friends and relatives in public. I was not to learn his true name until the funeral, when, according to Romany custom, it would be pronounced aloud in the prayer of pardon.

Stephen's nervousness became acute and he refused to cooperate with the health care plan. Despite the nurses' efforts to prevent him from having tobacco, he somehow managed several puffs a day before the cigarette could be taken away from him. According to his medical history, he had started smoking at the age of three months, or thereabouts, at his mother's breast. He would die smoking.

Medical histories not only permit health care teams to know where the patient's body has been injured by accident and disease, and how the body responded and repaired itself, but also where styles of living subject one's body to excessive strain. "Cigarette Smoking Is Dangerous To Your Health," and of course the resident ordered "No smoking." Medical histories may give clues to the ways organisms respond or react to pollution, accident, and disease. And the Surgeon General may have determined on the basis of a great number of medical histories that smoking is physiologically injurious to health. But he has not yet determined the injurious psychological consequences of abrupt disruption of a life style. Stephen's anxiety and aggressiveness lowered noticeably when he smoked.

The attending physician requested a psychiatric consultation with the patient. The psychiatrist reported:

> Patient exhibits denial. Practicing Roman Catholic [sic] who seems obsessed with his own immortality. Talks about going on a journey to get away from it all. Seems confused as to place and time of trip. Presence of visitors seems to accentuate condition.

Visitors had been restricted, but because of the large hospital population a few Gypsies always managed to get into the patient's room. Even small children managed to visit. As the health care staff more and more found themselves in an adversary position, the Gypsies began to be antagonistic and destructive. Finally they were confronted by the head of hospital security. One of the Gypsies assumed the role of spokesman. He announced that the patient was the "Gypsy King's son" and the visitors were his followers who had a right to be with him. In contrast to the aloof, antagonized, and disdainful attitudes which had been expressed toward him by the health care staff, the patient was now stereotyped as "the Gypsy prince." Nurses fluttered in and out of his room. Doctors came to examine and reexamine him. Even the hospital administrator managed to see what the "distinguished visitor" needed, and he ordered that one whole waiting room be reserved for the Gypsies on the ground floor. That helped with security, anyway, because the whole group could be watched by closed-circuit TV! Stephen had previously been treated as a hostile patient by the health care staff. Now he was receiving the top care of the house.

The stereotype, with its own perception of "history," functioned in a new way. Staff began reporting that hospital equipment disappeared and that the waiting room looked like a "pig's sty." After the Gypsies departed, the head of security confessed that the missing equipment had "mysteriously reappeared" or was found in the hospital's repair shops where it had been sent several weeks before the patient's arrival. He could think of nothing reported missing which could be attributed to the Gypsies' fingers.

But the stereotype functioned both for the benefit of the patient, who received better care, and for the Gypsies as a whole, who used the staff's predisposed assumptions about them to advantage. No *gadje* came into the "sty," and that meant the Gypsies could be themselves. The *gadje*'s attitude turned from one of disdain to one of fear, which meant that only "authorities" communicated with them. And that gave them a sense of importance, negative as it was, which is always better in such situations than to be ignored.

Despite all of the privileged treatment given the patient, visitors were still restricted from entering his room, with the exception of the group's spokesman. And the patient continued to be uncooperative and aggressive. A multidisciplinary team was organized to reinterview the patient. We began the interview by asking the patient which of his needs were not being met in the hospital. He replied that he wanted more tobacco because he wasn't "so nervous" when he smoked.

Question: "What is it that makes you nervous?"

Response: "Everything about this here place."

Question: "Can you think of anything else that might calm you?"

Response: "I need my people here."

Question: "You need your people here in your room to help you be calm?"

Response: "Yes."

Question: "The nurses have told us that you seem more nervous when you have visitors. Is that the case?"

Response: "I'm nervous when *gadje* are here. And I'm nervous when my people are kicked out. We can't be natural together."

For a Gypsy, whose identity is so deeply established as a member of a corporate people, to be separated from them at any time of crisis is a threat to his security. Upon recommendation of the interviewing team, the patient was moved next to a sizeable waiting room where the Gypsies could circulate in and out of the patient's room.

The psychiatrist had been correct in describing the patient as "exhibiting denial." That was objectively correct, but it led to an erroneous conclusion and an unsatisfactory health care plan. What happened after the patient's move is a good example of the "subjective" use often made of "denial." For the next few days the Gypsies circulated in and out, encouraging the patient to be ready for his "trip." What became obvious was that the "trip" referred to the journey across the River which encircles the world as the *Rom* know it—a view similar to the myth of Charon and the River Styx. What the psychiatrist had taken as a sign of "denial" of the patient's physical condition was instead the symbolic reference to the patient's destiny, for which appropriate preparation was vital. The hospital's procedures and the staff's ignorance of his contexts of reference thwarted the patient in his attempt to face the reality of his situation.

Appropriate preparation for the Gypsies included giving to the patient messages to be carried to loved ones "across the River." "When you see Baba's family, tell them we're okay." Baba's family had been killed in an auto accident several years previously. Death was that barrier beyond which harrassment and evil could no longer penetrate. Preparation also required saying goodbye to all of the relatives, settling disputes, entrusting the wife and children to others' care, and dividing responsibilities among the strong. As each of these concerns was cared for, the language of "denial" was used less and less.

Finally, at the end, all of the *Rom* pushed into Stephen's room so that his departing spirit could be assured that it was still among their people and so that their presence would be remembered and carried to the *Rom* beyond. Gypsies had come from all directions to be there for the precious moment when the world of release and union touched the world of oppression and separation in the passing of one of their people.

The *Rom* know themselves as "man" among "strangers." Much that exemplifies evil comes to them through strangers. To have surrounded the patient at the end with *gadje*, busy taking pulse or performing heroic measures for sustaining vital signs, would have prevented the patient from being with his people. It would have been understood by him as "hell." A sensitive report on his medical chart was: "The patient needs to die among his own kind."

When hospital procedures thwarted the Gypsies' rituals, the patient and his people tended toward panic. They feared that they would not be able to accomplish what is, for them, vital if one is to die correctly. They feared loss of control. Their sense of "dignity" required rituals they deemed necessary to complete one's destiny. "Denial," in multiple forms, was a ritualized attempt to hold off time long enough to complete the patient's business with his people.

Each person receives from his culture the stories of identity which give him the symbols by which he explains where he came from (myth of origin), where he is going (myth of destiny), and how he is to get there (myth of vocation). An individual discovers the boundaries of his identity through participation in the cultural rituals of his people which reveal paradigmatic models for thought and action. I understand ritual to mean habits of thought and action which themselves become symbolic and which relate persons to their people's myths of origin and destiny. Rituals not only reveal but permit access to that "right order" which creates and fulfills life's end. "End" when understood in the sense of the Greek word "telos" refers to purpose of destiny or fulfillment of design. Insofar as individual's behavior is rooted in the identity of a people, meaning for the individual is assessed by him on how well he has met the requirements of his people's destiny, for example, whether he has reached that development of life expected of the mature man. "End" when understood in the sense of the Latin word "finis" refers to termination or cessation. It is not a contradiction for man to seek a *telos* yet accept his *finis*. From his people's "subjective" history—the history they have either symbolized or remembered as meaningful—he drew his sense of propriety which was rooted in the hidden history of symbolic life.

The funeral took place in an old, somewhat shabby funeral parlor in the middle of the city. Unlike some of the funerals staged for publicity reasons, or others for which admission to journalists is charged, no *gadje* were permitted, except the funeral directors, the members of the brass band, and members of the clergy. Standing outside, seeing as much as she could, one onlooker observed, "These is sure strange people; nobody knows who they is or where they comes from." And that is the way the *Rom* intended it to be. Some minorities have believed that to be understood by the majority is to be accepted by them. That has never been the experience of the Gypsy, though he has tried several times in his long history. What he has learned is that his survival as a people depends upon his ability to remain inscrutable.

The corpse was never left alone. And while tears were shed, profusely so, crying was discouraged in the presence of the corpse. To do so might startle the spirit and disorient it for its journey.

Gypsies are ritual-conscious and adhere to the ways of their fathers. But they survive by being flexible with their surroundings. The rituals of the funeral reenacted the *Rom*'s self-understanding and their notions of destiny. As soon as the body was prepared for viewing, the relatives gathered for the wake, "to keep the spirit company."

Activity inside the funeral parlor was bedlam. There was loud talking broken by occasional laughter. Men swapped stories and women gossiped. With each new arrival the men greeted each other with virile embraces that would give WASP males a sexual identity crisis. Around the hallway and in the various rooms the floors were cluttered with debris: beer and soda cans, wine bottles, cigar and cigarette butts, crusts of bread, and food scraps left over from the huge feast with which the Gypsies had broken their fast when word came that one of their number had died. Strung along the buffet tables every couple of feet were onions crossed by leeks. Asked why they did this, the Gypsies answered, "We don't remember exactly. But we've always done it this way." Interspersed between items of gossip and tears of shock, someone would lean close to the ear of the deceased and in a mixture of English, Romany, and Slavic shout messages that had not been given to Stephen at the hospital. Above the casket was a big red banner which read, "Welcome To Heaven." The body was dressed as it probably never was in life—in formal morning attire. Even the hat was placed on the casket pillow. Stephen was off on his most important journey. The attire appears to be a recent adaptation of the American *Rom* yet it conforms with the Orthodox rubric, "Then the body is clothed in new garments, which symbolize our new garment of incorruption."

When Gypsies spent their entire life out-of-doors, they often refused to hold a funeral under a roof, even in a church. And the only decor they used, beside a box, was what nature provided. But now that they spend most of the year in a city, they have adopted the ways of the *gadje*. Morning attire, expensive water-tight caskets, embalming, and formal flower arrangements (sometimes made in Hong Kong) are all recent adaptations to Gypsy ritual. Like so many things they borrow from other cultures, however, the adaptations take on a symbolism strictly Gypsy and are made to fit into their scheme of living. The purpose of cosmetic embalming, according to the funeral trade magazines, is "to create a living memory picture so that those who come to pay their respects can remember their loved ones as they were." The Gypsy could not care less about any "living memory picture." But he does care about the shock to the spirit on being separated from its body. The contradiction between preparing the spirit for its journey and dressing the corpse in traveling clothes bothers the Gypsy not one bit. And it fits his understanding of death so well that he sets aside the traditional objections to having *gadje* touch one of their own.

Again, the Gypsy makes use of American funeral practice for his own advantage. To the Gypsy, a corpse is "unclean"; when the relatives prepared the body for burial it took a cleansing ritual which could last for several months to remove the taint. Some Gypsies in former times, knowing that they were about to die, would struggle into their "travelin' togs" so that their relatives could be spared the ordeal of touching the body. Even today, if there is sufficient warning, the dying Gypsy will move out of his house so as not to contaminate it.

When the priest arrived, the children were shooed out of his way. And the noise of chatter gave way to the sonorous richness of the liturgical chants. Cigarette smoke was soon replaced by burning incense, lifting the prayers up to God. At the priest's side stood the mother of the deceased, very much in charge of the funeral. "Ask God to let my boy's spirit stay with me a while before the journey," she demanded. And for the prayer of pardon, she gave the priest her son's true name—one of the few times it had been spoken aloud since his birth. "Don't let the Devil have your name and he'll never call you," goes an old Gypsy proverb. And neither Devil, policeman, Internal Revenue agent, or Selective Service officer ever gets a Gypsy's true name.

With one of the funeral's many incongruities, the richness of the priest's voice was soon followed by the tin blare of a three-piece band. Following the mother's downbeat, the musicians played "Rock-A-Bye Baby" and other favorite tunes of the deceased. They played "Autumn Leaves" and the mother began to sing to her deceased son. Then she danced with the open stance for which the Gypsy is famous.

As soon as everyone seemed satisfied that it was time to move to the Cathedral, the coffin was closed. But it was reopened after an argument between the brothers and the undertakers to make sure everyone knew the head and the foot ends of the coffin. "Ya messed it up last time, ya remember," one of the brothers said to the funeral director. He referred to a previous funeral in which the body had been carried out the door head first. That created such an outburst from the ritually sensitive Gypsies that the coffin had to be brought back indoors and the leave-taking begun over again.

When the coffin was outside, the women joined arms and formed a human cross behind the pallbearers, a practice apparently picked up when the *Rom* began to profess Christian beliefs. But a remnant of an even earlier purification rite was performed by the mother, who tossed cups of water along the path on which the coffin had been carried. Any old container seems to be appropriate. At this funeral one of the women had brought her plastic mop bucket, and paper cups were used as dippers. Once the coffin had been placed inside the funeral coach, the remaining contents of the bucket were thrown over the rear of the hearse. The water had neutralized the power of death which would otherwise have separated the deceased from his people by contaminating the ground over which death had passed.

The *Rom* had been obsessively sensitive in their obedience to rituals. This is not to say that they had not deviated from some of their fathers' customs, nor that all Gypsy wakes are exact copies of the one described, though the form is very similar. It is to say that they have a sense that they had done what was proper, had maintained a relationship with their fathers by reenacting their history, had perpetuated the distinctive character of their people by repeating their drama of destiny.

The funeral procession moved from the funeral parlor to the Russian Orthodox Cathedral. License plates on the cars indicated that Gypsies had come from as far away as Alabama, California, Florida, Texas, and Ontario. In the Cathedral, the coffin was left open throughout the service. After the Requiem had been sung, the oils administered, and the Ikon offered to the congregation, each of the *Rom* filed past the coffin. Most of them embraced the corpse, a seemingly spontaneous gesture. Children generally followed the suggestion simply to wave goodbye. As each man filed past the coffin, he pressed money into the hands of the deceased. Most left dollar bills, but some offered five- and even twenty-dollar bills. As the coffin was closed, now for the final time, a coin was placed in the teeth of the corpse—to pay the dread boatman who ferries souls across the River.

The funeral procession picked up a sound truck which played music all the way to the cemetery. The truck was an ordinary advertising van, its billboards reading "Jeansville U.S.A. Best deal in town. Three pairs for $14.95." It made for a splendid show. All along the way, *gadje* stopped in their tracks to stare.

At the cemetery, while the pallbearers and funeral directors were going through ritualized bickering and bargaining, the rest of the Gypsies proceeded to the open grave. With the health care staff, the clergy, the funeral directors, with every *gadje* whose services they needed, the *Rom* bargained vigorously. As lacking in decorum as this may seem to *gadje*, to the Gypsy it is crucial. How else to be perfectly clear about what can be expected? Bargaining with *gadje* is the only trusted way of relating for the *Rom*. And even then, they want constant assurance that the bargain will be honored.

After the priest had completed the prayers the vault top was put in place, sealed, and lowered into the ground. A number of coins were tossed in after it. One of the brothers brought a sizeable bundle of Stephen's clothes and possessions. Sometimes the possessions are passed around to be admired before being placed in the grave.

To many *gadje* the Gypsy appears very materialistic. But he usually acquires only what he can use, sometimes legally and sometimes otherwise. And at death, the really valuable possessions are buried with their owner. The roots of this practice seem to lie less with the notion that possessions can be taken into Heaven than with the notion that the spirit needs to be comforted by objects familiar to it from life.

Some *Rom* still practice the custom of giving most of the deceased's clothes to poor *gadje*. This is not an altruistic gesture. It is a hedge by the relatives against being bothered by an angry spirit which comes back to haunt the living. Supposedly the spirit would torment the body inside its former clothes!

With the earthly possessions in the grave, wagons of dirt were pulled alongside the grave and emptied. At one recent funeral a cement mixer was also used to help seal the grave. Apparently the concrete vault was thought to be adequate. The *Rom* know by long experience that the graves of their deceased are a great temptation for robbers; short of being abandoned by their own people, nothing is more repugnant to them. Though they have probably never read the story, they know firsthand what motivated Antigone.

Once the sod was in place the Gypsy men brought out the iced beer and soda. While one of the brothers poured libations of brandy over the grave the rest of the *Rom* poured out some of their drinks. To one side, careful not to let her hem cover the grave, Stephen's mother did a little dance while she sang "Autumn Leaves." Before the great funeral feast could begin, however, there were other graves to be visited. As one of the relatives knocked on the headstone yelling out the name of the deceased, the priest would say a short prayer of comfort, should the spirit still be in residence. Some of the relatives would be on all fours and would yell messages. For a year, on ritual days, special food would be brought to the graves for the spirit: should it not yet have begun its journey, it could be comforted. The widow would ritually mourn, avoiding other men and doing no dancing. The family would not refer to the deceased by any name, so as not to call the spirit back. Separated from its body, the *Rom* believe, the spirit is even more vulnerable to evil until it crosses the River.

On the anniversary of the death the *Rom* came together for a great feast. At the head of the table there was a chair, sometimes empty, sometimes filled by one who wore the clothes of the deceased. Anyone who had unfinished business with the deceased raised the matter. Finally the widow, in almost liturgical rhythm, reported to the spirit how she had remained faithful to him for the whole period of mourning. Then, in the eyes of the *Rom*, everything proper with respect to the deceased had been done. The period of dying was over. The mourning period was over. And they had a blast!

The *Rom* had acted out their myths of destiny. Until this is understood their sense of origin, vocation, and numbers are inscrutable. When they are asked about their origin, they may give a place name in order to satisfy their *gadje* questioners. But for them, origin was the beginning of their *telos*, and the *Rom*'s *telos* is to survive as a people. When they are asked about their numbers, they give as exaggerated a figure as they dare, and many social scientists have believed them. But when they speak among themselves of numbers, they talk about birth rate, the need to keep the race alive, and the need for more hands to make money. Only then can the people survive.

Both their symbolic life and their memories of the past tell of a trail of persecution so vicious that they, unlike majority peoples, have never been permitted to settle long enough to acquire an identity located in geography. And consequently they hold no hope of becoming a majority people anywhere. Between 300,000 and 500,000 *Rom* were exterminated in the ovens of Nazi Germany. The word "Nazi" for many *Rom* has replaced the Romany word for Devil. But the Nazi pogroms were unusual only in intensity and numbers. Many of their people were still slaves in Eastern Europe at the time of Lincoln's Emancipation Proclamation. Most of their people are still harassed nearly every place they go.

The "objective" histories about the *Rom* tell of hoards of beggars, swindlers, and thieves spreading over Europe and the Americas. The "subjective" histories of the *Rom* remember a trail of persecution and oppression. The case histories about the *Rom* tell of unemployment, welfare checks, and poverty. The *Rom*'s own memory speaks of imagination, cleverness, and luck in vocations which permitted him to survive. The medical histories tell about the Gypsy's diseases and vices. The *Rom*'s own record is of disease and evil conquered.

The question of an ethnic group's identity seems to be argued on the old distinction of "objectivity vs. subjectivity." The objective perspective permits us to see relationships in space and time. But taken by itself it permits the prejudices of the majority to be reinforced within their own frames of reference. True, the subjective perspective gives us the prejudiced frames of reference of the minority. But only the subjective perspective gives us the meaning of history as the ethnic group itself sees it. Not understanding the meaning of history for them, we diminish the minority people's sense of identity through our efforts to objectify and quantify. Sometimes accurately, but more times not, our efforts to objectively understand others melts them into the pot of our own making. And their true history remains hidden to us. At least this is what the *Rom* have revealed to me. And it may also have revealed that my efforts to objectify and quantify my own history at the expense of what I have taken my past to mean, have diminished my own identity.

NOTES

1. The most extensive and reliable source of information is the *Journal of the Gypsy Lore Society*, which has been issued in three series. The first series began in 1888.
2. Richardson Wright, "Gypsy Lore in America: 1888-1938," *JGLS*, Third Series, XVII, No. 3, p. 12.
3. Allan Pinkerton, *The Gypsies and the Detectives* (New York, 1879) p. 69.

THE DEVELOPMENT OF ETHNIC IDENTIFICATIONS AMONG THIRD-GENERATION JAPANESE AMERICANS

MAGOROH MARUYAMA

M OST OF THE THIRD-GENERATION descendants of the original Japanese immigrants in the U.S.A. have now reached the age level of adolescence and young adulthood. The third-generation Japanese Americans are called "Sanseis" (the first generation are called "Isseis," and the second generation "Niseis").

The environments in which the Sanseis grew up are diverse: many grew up in predominantly Black communities; others in predominantly white communities, still others in racially mixed communities; some moved between several types of communities, and some stayed in one community as it changed in its racial composition.

Of those born in Black communities, many developed an identification with Blacks while others withdrew from their Black neighbors. Those born in mixed (Black and white) communities tended to feel that each side categorized them with the other, or compelled them to choose between sides. Of those born in white communities there are those who strove to be "white" as well as those who remained Japanese. In adolescence many changed their pattern of ethnic association and "discovered" new races whom they had excluded in their child-

Mr. Maruyama was born in Japan, studied in Germany, Denmark, and Sweden, and has been on the faculties of the University of California at Berkeley, Stanford University, Brandeis University, and Antioch College. This paper is based on written autobiographies by Sansei students enrolled in Asian American study courses in San Francisco Bay Area colleges during the 1969-1970 academic year.

hood associations (in some cases the Japanese race itself had been excluded in childhood association). Then a new choice was made, in one of a number of directions. The patterns are individual.

The following study is based on autobiographic materials written by the Sanseis who were in an Asian American Community Study Project in the East Bay area near San Francisco. Most of them grew up in the Bay area or the Los Angeles area; a small number grew up in Hawaii, the Midwest, or the Rocky Mountain area. The project included students of Chinese and Filipino as well as Japanese background. Their experiences are strikingly similar, and the Japanese and the Chinese experiences are interchangeable except for some intra-ethnic details. The Filipino experiences are somewhat different in two respects: Filipinos are often mistaken as Chicanos or Blacks; and most of the Filipinos are Catholics.

There was a total of approximately 30 Sanseis and some Isseis (young immigrants or students who have recently come from Japan). The autobiographies of several of them were chosen for discussion in this article. The choice was made in order to cover a wide range of experiences. One young Issei is included for comparison.

The importance of these autobiographies lies in their phenomenological quality, which enables the reader to view the culture from the in-culture perspective. They should not be taken as merely "clinical" material, if "clinical" is meant to be dealing with individuals who are "malfunctioning," "maladapted," "maladjusted," or "suffering" because of their "personal" problems, who are "abnormal" and are therefore not "average" and "healthy" people in the population. The writers of these autobiographies are representative, ordinary members of an ethnic group. The "problems" presented here are cultural and social rather than individual. However, they are *not* cultural "problems" in the sense of abnormal cases reflecting cultural factors (such as in cross-cultural psychiatry); *nor* are they social "problems" in the sense of delinquency or deviance. They manifest social and cultural situations affecting the entire ethnic group which is under pressure from the dominant society. The purpose of this article is to present some of the effects of this pressure in detail.

Patti Nakanishi

I can distinctly remember the first blow as being considered "different" from the white kids. It all started in kindergarten. During the first few weeks I endured the physical strain of grammar school life. But within the third week or so, the kids would come up to me and ask me, "Why are you different? Why do you have a flat nose?" I replied, "I don't have a flat nose!" Then I ran to the restroom and observed in the mirror that my nose was considerably flat, just as the kids were saying. What a blow! That very same night I remember confronting my mother with uncontrollable crying, eyes flooding with tears, and endless whimpering and asked her, "Why do I have a flat nose?" She began to comfort me and told me, "You are of a different nationality, Japanese, and it's a physical characteristic of the Japanese to have a flat nose." Somehow I couldn't readily accept her explanation; I thought she was trying to hide the fact that I was a physically deformed kid. I realized from that day forward that I was different. I began to pair up with a Polish girl who couldn't speak English well, while the other kids laughed behind our backs as two "foreignly different" kids played together. As the year grew shorter the other kids became more tolerant and started including us in their games and fantasies.

In second grade I made friends with the only other Asian kid in the whole school. She was a new student, Chinese, but, like me, American-born. The teacher told me to show the new girl around school (mainly because we were of similar descent). From that day we became the closest of friends, even joined the same Brownie troop. I finally discovered that there were other Asians in the world, but still I couldn't understand why there were so few as compared to China Town or Japanese Town. It crushed me when my Chinese friend moved away later that year . . . there I would have to remain as the only Asian in school.

All through elementary school my nationality engulfed me because of the kids at school who would come up to me and slant their eyes with their fingers, chanting, "Ching, Chong, Chinaman!" I felt like going up to those kids and beating them up, "Don't you know the difference? I'm Japanese!"

When our family moved to Fremont from San Rafael in 1958,

I had a whole new outlook. I tried to consider myself as white. Everything would go fine until some "wise-acre" would come up and call me a "Chink" or "Jap." I lived in fantasy for a while; I would tell people I was neither Japanese nor Chinese—"I'm Outer Mongolian." It would hurt me to have little kids recognize me as something "different."

It became a pretty regular thing to be considered "different," so that finally it didn't faze me one bit. But my healing wounds were again reopened in fifth grade. I became good friends with a white school chum. I even started taking her to my Presbyterian Church. One day I went over to her house to pick her up to go to church. It was Easter Sunday. She came outside to greet me in her play clothes. There I was in my Easter dress expecting to see her show off her new Easter dress. She explained, "My mother won't let me to go church or even play with you ever again. She doesn't want me to associate with Orientals because she thinks I might marry one when I get older. She said she doesn't want me having anything to do with your kind. Please forgive her, Patti—she's crazy! My dad or I don't care who I associate with." I just shrugged my shoulders and started crying. I never felt so hurt in all my life.

After that incident I felt like concealing my whole culture. I just couldn't live on that way! I even started hating to walk with another Japanese, even my own cousins! I didn't want to be considered a Japanese after encountering such a horrible experience in the fifth grade. The episode of my girlfriend's mother's prejudice affected me psychologically for many years to come. Anybody who looked at me in the slightest way would receive a shattered look of agony from me. I kept my head looking down at the ground most of the time when walking through the school halls or in a streetful of people. By the seventh grade I was psychologically warped! I thought my seventh grade Core teacher was prejudiced toward "yellow meat" because every time he would speak about Chinese Communists he seemed to accusingly look at me, as if I were a Chinese Communist . . . as a result of this, I did very poorly in my studies. My persecution complex was subdued the next year, in the eighth grade, when I had the same teacher and we got along marvelously that year; in fact, I received a scholastic award in his class. Also in the eighth grade I received a broken

nose playing basketball with four balls. This broken nose somewhat raised my plateau nose a bit; I felt that now that I had
a "not-as-flat" nose I could be more easily accepted as a white
(crazy childish thinking).

I can remember becoming interested in boys. My parents
warned me to be careful because some parents wouldn't want
their son to be going around with an Asian. I couldn't believe
that people could be so narrow-minded; but I realized that
it was true when my brother started dating Caucasian girls.
Three times he had to break up with girls because of their
parents' attitude toward a mixed relationship. I started to be
hesitant toward boys because of this situation.

As a Junior in high school, I tried out for yell leader. I desper-
ately went through all of the old high school yearbooks, hoping
to find an Asian spirit leader. No luck! I began thinking that
I won't be able to become one because of my nationality. It
was an ego-booster when I was selected as a yell leader. No
matter how hard I tried, I couldn't seem to get away from
the fact I was Japanese. As a Senior, I still was involved as
a yell leader . . . that year I was nominated for Homecoming
Queen! To add to the surprise, the first runner-up was a
Chinese-white girl, Mary Leith. Mary and I joked each other
through our Senior year and based our honored positions to
our Oriental Mystique. This award brought me out of my persecution syndrome. However, I still didn't really want to
associate with "my" people.

It wasn't until the second quarter in college that I realized
I shouldn't be ashamed of my heritage. I discovered that a
person can't be beautiful until he is proud of his culture. I
think I have reached a level of understanding with myself—I
am proud of my ancestry and what I am.

AUDREY NOBORI

I am the last born of the four children in my family. We're
all spaced three years apart. Since before I was born we've
had a housekeeper that came to our house at 8:00 a.m. and
stayed until 6:00 p.m. She got us ready for school and fixed
lunch and dinner for us. I, being the youngest, was very close
to her and she was my shield of protection from my sisters.
Ever since I was a tot I was always fairly close to my brother,
who was six years older than I. I lived in South Berkeley, which

was predominantly Black, and attended Lincoln Elementary School. When I first started school a few of the children called me "Ching, Chong, Chinaman" but they soon accepted me. All my friends were Black and I rarely saw any white or other Asian kids. I really didn't understand any difference in race as I remember, because our housekeeper was Black, except she was very fair-skinned and I didn't see any difference between her and a white person. Besides that, I called her "Mama" and treated and reacted to her as if she really were my own mother. All of her children were grown and I used to get jealous of them to hear them call her "Mama" when I believed I had the right to call her that. Several of my Black friends were also light-skinned and I had difficulty distinguishing the difference because I rarely saw any white kids. We formed our little crowd and I just fit right in. I didn't even think of myself as looking any different from them. We all had our little kindergarten boyfriends, and as I recall mine was Mexican, then later a Black. Later, in third grade, a white family moved in the neighborhood and the kids went to Lincoln. We beat them up at every recess and called them "white patties." The term "rice patty" was never used on me, only it was converted to "white" instead of "rice" to mock the white children. I learned to hate the white children as did the Blacks but I had no reason—only that my friends didn't like them so I didn't either. The white family moved out of the neighborhood after two weeks. I attended Lincoln School up through the third grade. I had several friends, all of whom were Blacks. I had no acquaintances with whites or other Asians. I only saw Asian kids while I was at church. Our church had a white pastor.

With a Black housekeeper, we were exposed to foods such as mustard greens, hamhocks, and other food known as soul food. We put butter on our rice since that's how the Blacks did.

For recreation, my father liked water sports and owned a boat, so we often went water skiing. Other families, whites, usually went with us.

In the fourth grade we moved, and it was necessary for me to transfer to Jefferson School, where there were mostly white children. Asians outnumbered Blacks. I was very unhappy at this school because the white kids made me feel uncomfortable. As a new student I was extra lost, because everyone seemed to know everyone else in the class. My first friend was a Japanese girl. This girl was not too popular with the other kids, but she was very nice to me. I spoke differently from the kids at this school because I had picked up the Blacks' usage of the language, with slang often used. I was embarrassed to speak at this school because everyone else, even the few Blacks, spoke beautiful English and I spoke as if I lived in a ghetto.

There was one crowd I wanted to be in very much, but the leader, a Japanese girl, was really rude to me. She was much bigger than I and really a "meanie." This group seemed to be closer to what I was used to than any other, because the only Black girl was in this crowd. In slang expression, this group seemed to have "soul" and all the other "honkies" (whites) were foul! The Japanese girl that was my friend was really "sweet," but I was used to roughing it. I made friends next with the Black girl and I really liked her because she could speak my language. In other words, I could use the lingo I was used to and we'd communicate really good! The Black girl allowed me to play with them at recess and stuff, although the leader didn't want any part of me. As time went by, I won the friendship of everyone in that crowd except the Japanese leader. She really hated me, but she began to lose her throne, in a sense, because all the others were getting tired of her being so mean to me. Finally we became friends, and I at last felt comfortable with this crowd. The fact that so many white kids went there still bothered me, but I knew mostly all of the Blacks that attended and mixed with them. All my after school activity was with them.

In my sixth grade class a boy (Black) that I had gone to Lincoln School with was in my class. It made me homesick because we always talked about old times and all the kids back there. I wrote quite often to my best friend there. In junior high I started mingling with other Asians that mixed primarily with Blacks. At this time the Black influence was bad on me. This particular group always got into trouble. It was a test to see how effective the law was, or something. I saw so much stealing and petty theft that I decided I didn't want this any more and decided to change my outlook on life. I then decided that in the future I'd like to be a probation officer for juvenile delinquents. I began to take school a little more seriously and wanted to meet more Asians, so I joined the Berkeley Bears

Youth Organization, which consisted of all Japanese and had basketball and baseball teams. Through this I met many Asians. I continued this through high school. All ninth graders went to one school so I met up with several of my old friends. I also met many older Chinese boys. These boys were about four or five years older than I, but I went out with them and we became very good friends. Later in high school I began to really feel the different racial groups. Berkeley is so integrated that in the high school every different group was in one and were easy to pick out. The group most hated by the Asians was the social clubs. White upper-middle-class. We had hippies and Blacks. It was in high school that Asian identity became important to me. I hated the Oriental who tried to be "in" with the Whites. Our Asian group called these few "White Japs." In high school, our Asian group was accepted by the Blacks and often we passed Blacks exchanging the "Black Power" salutation of raising the fist.

After high school I wanted to go to Los Angeles where the Asian population is greater. Complications in moving forced me to come to Cal State where there are nothing but whites, and I cannot mix successfully with whites. After I started, I found it very difficult to make friends. My girlfriend and I decided to join the Ski Club where we met many friendly whites and I changed my outlook on the white people. I've attended several parties where I had a lot of fun. I've been experimenting with them in a sense for the past year. I've gone steady with one and have become very good friends with others. I've interviewed a few of them and have found that they differ a lot.

. . . .

One white boy I dated said something about a "nigger." I asked him, "Don't you like Blacks?" He said very quickly, "No, I hate 'em." I said, "Why?" He hesitated a bit and said, "They're just good for nothing and wanna take over." I said, "Boy, you're really prejudiced, huh?" He said, "Yeah, I hate Blacks." I said, "Well, I'm just the same as a Black, are you prejudiced against me?" He said, "No, you're not, your're different, I don't think of you as being different from me!" I said, "I identify myself with the Blacks, therefore, I'm the same as a Black, and if you don't like the Blacks, then you must be prejudiced against me." At this time he was very frustrated and was getting angry. The subject was making him edgy. I saw the anger through his driving, he was getting a little reckless! To top things off, I said, "Well, don't get mad just because you're prejudiced and get into an accident and kill me!" That made him think a little. He slowed down and a little calmer, "I don't see why you identify yourself with the Blacks, because I don't see the link." I told him, "Minority power, power to the people; we've been discriminated against as the Blacks have." He said, "I really wasn't aware that you were discriminated against." I said, "Yeah," and dropped the subject.

· · · · · · · · · ·

This past year, I've learned so much about the different types of people. My parents would like to see me mingle with more Asians but I tell them I'm learning so much about the white people and they're beginning to understand me. They want me to eventually marry an Asian but I told my mom I don't think I will. In our family tree, two are married to whites, two are married to Chinese, and two are married to Japanese. Four of us have white boyfriends or girlfriends, two Chinese, and the rest are still looking.

LARRY KOBORI

When I was young I noticed I was a little different from my friends. My father told me I was Japanese and that I should never be ashamed of being Japanese. He has emphasized this for as long as I can remember.

I don't remember ever experiencing any racial prejudice from my friends or from their parents. But watching television I saw war movies where "the only good Jap was a dead Jap." This was my first encounter with the word "Jap." I knew it was bad by the way John Wayne kept saying it. The "Japs" supposedly killed Wayne's friend but it's strange that Hollywood showed only the Japanese soldiers being shot. I was glad that my friends never called me a "Jap."

When I started school everything was perfect until the fourth grade. Some kids called me a "Chink." I told them I'm Japanese, not Chinese. If I was going to be called a dirty name at least use the proper dirty name. My friends always told me to forget those kids, that those kids were stupid. I was glad to hear my friends say that.

I played second base on my fourth-grade softball team. Every once in a while if I threw someone out or caught a fly ball a guy would say something like, "Hey, Jap, why didn't you drop the ball?" or something like, "Hell, I made an out to the Jap." When this happened my friends would always tell me to forget it.

After a while the fourth grade things straightened out. But in the seventh grade we started to read about World War I and World War II. I knew that in World War II Japan attacked Pearl Harbor. So I worked real hard on World War I. I answered every question I could. But when it came to World War II, I never answered any questions. I would just slouch in my chair. I guess I was feeling ashamed and embarrassed at the atrocities of Japan during World War II. But what I didn't understand was why the textbooks and the teacher glorified America's bombing of Hiroshima and Nagasaki. My teacher said thousands of civilians, including women and children, were killed by the atom bombs, thus making Japan surrender. She then added that the bombings had saved many American lives. I then asked my teacher, "Wouldn't that be considered an atrocity since so many civilians died? That's the way you describe Japanese atrocities." I'll never forget the way she stared at me and said, "There's a difference." Today that episode is still clear as a bell. It's something that I've never forgotten.

In junior high I can't remember anything that happened at school. But one year during the Christmas season I was in line to buy something when the manager or some store employee pushed me out of line and let a white man in my spot. I went back in the line ahead of this guy when the manager and a security cop pulled me back out and told me to get at the end of the line. I protested and said that the man cut in front of me. The cop said, "Get at the end of the line or else I'll send you back to China." I noticed that everyone was looking and giving me weird looks so I went to the end of the line. That was in the ninth grade and after that I made a promise to myself never to let that kind of thing happen again. I wasn't going to let anyone take advantage of me any more.

My three years in high school were the best years. I felt that now I was really being accepted. I was the varsity scorekeeper for three years in football, basketball, and baseball. I couldn't compete on the high school level so I did what I could to help. I learned the plays and found myself getting to know the other guys much better. I was then encouraged to write sport stories in the local newspaper. When these stories came out the sophs and juniors wanted me to help them. As a result I got to know quite a few of them.

There were only three Japanese in my senior class, all boys. When the Senior Ball came around my Japanese friend and I dated white girls. When nobody seemed to care my friend and I both agreed that we had been completely accepted. I felt I had been accepted because the other students knew me as a person.

Outside of class sometimes it was a different story. Traveling with the basketball team, some Blacks called me a "Jap." Remembering my promise I turned around and was about to call the Blacks "Niggers." I restrained myself because I was sure it would lead to a fight. The same thing happened when some Mexicans called me a "Jap." Once again I refrained from retaliating. I'll never understand why those people called me a "Jap."

There was only one other incident that I can remember. I went to the public library for some magazines when this white man pointed at me, called me a "Jap" and laughed. This time I wasn't going to forget it. So I yelled at him and said, "What did you say?" The guy looked really startled; I don't think he was expecting me to make a scene. He mumbled back, "Nothing." I yelled back, "What did you say? Speak up!" Now the librarian starts walking over. But before she arrives the man walks out of the libary. I felt good after that. It was good to see that man turn about eight different shades of red. That has been my strategy ever since.

HIKARU ARAKI

When I came to this country, I was put in a white community. I lived with a middle-aged white couple. There were neither Asians nor Negroes in this area. Everything was new for me, and since I wanted to get used to the American way of life I imitated Americans and acted like Americans; I almost forgot that I was a Japanese.

One day, as we were eating dinner, the husband said to me, "I am telling you because I don't want you to be embarrassed when you are invited for dinner by somebody, but don't make any noise when you eat." The way he said it sounded very sarcastic to me. In Japan making noise when you eat radishes or carrots means that you are enjoying eating. I realized that I was different from them. Before I went to bed, I looked at my face in the mirror and I told myself that I am different.

Since my sponsors went to a Lutheran church, I started going to church with them. Members of this church were all whites, and they gave me an American name, Harry, so I felt that I was a white. When I was in the church, in the supermarket, and at the home, I didn't have any consciousness of being Japanese.

My sponsor had a relative close to where we lived, so I often visited them. One day they asked me if I had found a girlfriend at the school, and I said, "No." Then they said, "That's shame that there is no Japanese at your school." This statement shocked me and stopped my smiling. I realized that I had forgotten my nationality. Yes, I am a Japanese, but why does my girlfriend have to be a Japanese? Why can't I go out with a white girl? I was mad at them, and at the same time I started hating myself for being a Japanese. I wanted to be a white. I knew nobody could do anything about it, but I couldn't help it.

A few days after this the family and I went to the shopping center, where we met a Japanese American girl. She was their daughter's classmate and was a cheerleader. She was a very attractive girl and they suggested that I take her out. But I felt, If I keep myself away from other Japanese, then they won't categorize me as a Japanese. So I didn't want to associate with other Japanese. I just said to them, "I rather like a blond-haired girl." They looked at me strangely and said nothing.

A few months after, I started working at a pizza parlor. I knew it was an odd place for a Japanese to work, but it was not odd for a Japanese American. Many customers gave strange stares at me, as if they were saying that this was the wrong place for me to work. One day when I was taking orders at the counter, a middle-aged man thought I was a Chinese. He said, "Give me a chop suey." I said, "I am sorry, sir, we don't have chop suey here." Then he raised his voice, "Hah! you can't make chop suey?" I knew he was a little drunk, but I was mad. "Sir, I can make anything, but this is a pizza parlor. If you want chop suey, you can get it at Chinese restaurants."

His friend eased him out. Another day, another customer came to me: "Hey, you are not Italian, are you?" I said, "No, I am not." He asked, "What is your nationality?" I said, "I am a Japanese." He asked, "How come is a Japanese making pizza?" I asked, "Aren't you Italian?" He said, "No, I am a German." Finally, I said, "How come is a German eating pizza?" He said nothing but laughed awkwardly.

This pizza parlor has a pipe organ. On every Saturday night, an organist explained about musical instruments which belonged to this pipe organ. When it came to the Chinese cymbal, he always said, "Ah—So—." All the customers laughed so loudly. It sounded stupid to me. So I told the organist that "Ah—So—" was not Chinese but Japanese. I just wanted people to make a distinction between Chinese and Japanese. Since that time he stopped saying that.

I am proud of the economic prosperity and great history of Japan. I am proud of being Japanese. But whenever I am picked on, I feel that I wish I were a white.

JANET KIKUKO SANDERS

Never before have I seriously attempted to dissect my feelings and attitudes about myself as a Japanese American. Aborted attempts were made but never brought to final fruition. I suspect because certain truths about oneself are unbearably painful, I preferred to postpone my confrontation with reality until I was able to cope with the consequences of such a confrontation.

I am Japanese and there is no denying this. On the other hand, I am also American, not a white American, but a diluted, yellow-white one. I say yellow-white American, because no matter how hard I try to reject the values of the dominant white society, these very values remain ingrained in me. So much so that I am unconscious of their presence. This truth I have had to face in spite of my newly-found pride in ethnic origin. To accept myself as a total person I also have to accept the dual existence of Asian and American values in my life. For the modern Asian raised in the Asian American style, the struggle for a clear-cut identity is a very real dilemma, in spite of the similarities between the two cultures' value systems. My parents urged me, unconsciously I am certain, to perpetuate the stereotype of the quiet, polite, unassuming Asian. But survival in American society requires one to speak up vociferously to defend one's rights and gain recognition. Slowly I am rejecting the Asian stereotypes, in hopes that by doing so I am contributing to the elimination of the Asian stereotypes held by white America. A change in the attitudes of Caucasians toward Asians will not occur until we alter the attitudes we have toward ourselves.

Discrimination toward the Asian American today is usually so subtle that one of Asian ancestry may not be able to recognize prejudices at work. I am very sensitive to verbal and non-verbal reactions of whites to me. I have to be able to distinguish between discriminatory remarks and "non-color" remarks or actions. Asian Americans, much like Blacks, are on the defensive. Only after carefully examining each situation can we attribute an action or remark to prejudice. For example, if I fail to get a desired job, do I blame my failure on racial prejudice or on my own lack of ability? The circumstances of the situation must be considered before any conclusions are drawn. I feel I have experienced subtle discrimination, the kind of discrimination which is more difficult to detect, define and to cope with. While shopping at so-called "better stores," I have come into contact with rather aloof saleswomen who have treated me with cold indifference. I could almost sense their thinking, "What could she possibly want or afford in this store?" At first I felt their superior, haughty behavior was a reaction to the way I was dressed on those occasions. But no, even when I was properly attired, I was treated in like manner.

I have had similar experiences in restaurants where I have been treated indifferently and made to wait a bit longer. Once a friend and I had lunch at San Francisco's Fisherman's Wharf. I had chosen the Wharf because this particular friend was a first-time visitor to the city. We were seated and our orders were taken before those of the older white women who had come in after us. Well, those two white women were served before us. We noticed this but preferred to believe the waiter had had a slight mix-up of orders. I knew the oversight was not because our dishes took longer to prepare, as the women were having the same lobster dish I had ordered. When our meals arrived, they were overdone. I know I should have refused to accept the dishes but I remained silent as the waiter suspected I would. (Stereotype: Asians never complain; for that matter, most people don't.) My friend, when asked by the waiter upon completion of the meal if she had enjoyed it, replied, "Not really, it was overcooked."

I had a very painful experience while in Europe with my mother. People are always saying how tolerant the Europeans are of race, creed, and color. A Black friend told me about his wonderful experiences in Europe where he never encountered discrimination. I did, in Vienna, Austria. I was particularly aware of being constantly stared at—the staring was not always friendly. My unpleasant experience with the hotel concierge is still fresh in my memory. One morning before going out on a tour, I went to the hotel desk to use a pen to sign a traveler's cheque. I used the concierge's pen, then placed the pen on the desk. Mom and I left for the tour and returned several hours later. When I arrived at the desk, the concierge asked me brusquely, "May I have my pen back, please?" I told him I did not have it, as I distinctly remember returning it. But he was certain I had it on my person. He then asked me to check my handbag, which I did reluctantly; still no pen. I explained to him that I was not in the habit of stealing pens. He then said, "I had that pen for five years." Obviously, he did not believe me. I was never so insulted in my life. I am certain this man would never have approached any other hotel guest as he did me. He was either terribly rude and unwordly or he was just prejudiced. I believe it was the latter.

I think most Asian-Americans have experienced discrimination, overt or subtle, directed at them. I asked a number of my friends if they had ever been discriminated against. To my surprise they said no. This made me wonder if I was subtly harrassed because of my personality and not because of my color. I also wondered if I was being too sensitive and a bit paranoid. But knowing my friends led me to one conclusion: if they had encountered prejudice, they did not recognize it or they refused to recognize it. By recognizing prejudice directed at you, you are forced to look at yourself and what you are. You are compelled to see yourself as different, as a member of a minority group. Facing the truth can be a painful experience. You are not quite as white as the white society you wish to identify yourself with.

I have finally faced this reality. I am yellow—I cannot change what I am. I can say honestly now that I am proud of being Japanese. This pride is based upon our illustrious history as a people, our culture, and our undying spirit. Even as imprisoned peoples during World War II, the Japanese displayed courage and ethnic pride. My mother told me a great deal about her camp experiences. She fondly recalls the unity and high morale of the group during internment. As an act of defiance and also as an exercise in keeping the morale high, the Japanese in the Rivers, Arizona camp celebrated all of the traditional festivals and holidays of their native land by donning native costumes (kimonos, yukatas), dancing native dances, and eating traditional foods. Once, during the big New Year's celebration, a few daring young Japanese boys stealthily climbed a small hill within the compound and hoisted the flag of Japan emblazoned with the symbolic rising sun. The Army officials quickly removed it and demanded to know who put the flag up. They never found the culprits, The Japanese enjoyed the stunt immensely. This was just one incident my mother recounted. To my memory, my father, on the other hand, has never discussed his camp experiences. For a man, such involuntary imprisonment was an emasculating experience. The role of "breadwinner" and protector of the family was taken away from him. My dad will never again reside on the U.S. mainland; he prefers to remain in Hawaii, which boasts a large Asian population.

In spite of their internment during the war, my parents feel a sense of gratitude toward the U.S. For them the "American Dream" has been realized; they have enjoyed a modest success in their business, they have earned and saved enough for their dream home, they have purchased that second new car, and now they look forward to a life filled with more leisure and less struggle. I am happy for them, but for me such attainment is not enough. I feel that where real equality is concerned, we still have a long way to go. Unlike my parents I don't feel a sense of gratitude toward the U.S. What we have, we earned. We made our opportunities when there were none and capitalized on them.

I feel a common bond with my Asian brethren, whereas at one time I did not. As a Japanese raised in Hawaii, I looked upon the Asians on the U.S. mainland as a different breed. I felt they were too American because they thought, acted, and spoke like the Caucasian. I now realize this was an Island stereotype of the West Coast Asian. Also, if there is truth in the belief that the West Coast Japanese are stand-offish and less open and friendly, then it is probably due to their greater exposure to racial prejudice. The Japanese here have always been aware of their minority group status. Now that I reside in California and have Asian friends here, I find the Asians friendly, informed, and involved. I have changed; I am aware of our group's social problems as well as the problems of other minority groups. I identify with these minorities and feel that we need the strength of unity to attain our goals in this society, our goals being (1) recognition as individuals and not as stereotyped peoples; (2) equality, and (3) eradication of racial prejudice.

I am already looking forward to the day when I start my family. My husband, who is white, and I want our children to be proud of their Japanese-American heritage. Presently, we are tracing my family lines back to my Japanese ancestors in the old country hundreds of years ago. Then we will be able to pass on this valuable knowledge to our children. We want them to be familiar with the Japanese language and customs. Sadly, I, a third-generation Japanese in the U.S., have lost a great deal of the Japanese traditions. I wish I had paid closer attention to the traditional Japanese ways of my parents and grandparents. My mother told me years ago when I turned my back on things Japanese that one day I would regret not learning more about Japanese culture. She was right.

So, as inadequate a teacher as I may be, I will attempt to transmit to my children one day what little I have retained of my Japanese heritage. I hope our half-white, half-yellow children will be proud of being Japanese-American.

CONCLUSION

These autobiographies represent a part of a wide range of variations in ethnic identifications among the third-generation Japanese youths in the United States. The developmental paths of identifications vary individually: Some came through identification with Blacks, others through identification with whites, and still others without any strong identification. There is no predominant pattern of past identifications among the approximately thirty Sanseis who were in the project. One tentative inference one may make is that the pattern of friendship gratification or lack of gratification in early childhood has a strong influence on later identification.

If the paths of identifications vary, they nevertheless seem to converge to a realization of ethnic pride. This is seen in most of the students in the project.

Some of the Sanseis suffer from the logic of dichotomy instilled in them in the Western (American) culture. They reason that they have to be either American or Japanese, but cannot be both: since they don't speak Japanese and are not versed in the Japanese culture, they must be American; but they are not really American, etc. They get into a dilemma which is more an intellectual than a psychological conflict. This shows the degree of their Americanization. A native Japanese does not think in a dichotomous logic. For example, to a Japanese it is perfectly natural to go to a Shinto shrine for marriage, a Buddhist temple for funerals, and to celebrate Christmas. For a native Japanese the dichotomous question of identity does not arise.

Furthermore, the "problems" in these autobiographies are not endemic or intra-cultural: They are due to intercultural contact, and more precisely in most cases due to *the pressure from the dominant culture*. Though not included in this paper, which selected only Japanese examples, there is a Chinese student in our project who grew up in a Black community and who, though repeatedly rejected by Black children, persisted in his efforts in becoming accepted by Blacks, converted himself to the Black culture, and ended up as a super-Black (a successful pimp and hustler).

These examples show the traumatic and detrimental effects of the dominant culture, whatever color it happens to be, upon minority cultures. These effects are not a result of conscious design on the part of the members of the dominant culture. In fact, the members of the dominant culture are unaware of the effects they are creating, and this lack of awareness makes the solution of the problem much more difficult. When the problem is brought to the surface, the members of the dominant culture are likely to feel unjustly blamed, because they have had no awareness of their own "crime." The members of the dominant culture may therefore consider the grievance illogical and retaliate against the "illogical," "immature," or "immoderate" claims of the minority groups.

Until Black people began voicing their situation, most of the white community was unaware of the "problem," and after hearing the Black voices most of the white community started calling the situation a "Black problem" without realizing that it is a *white problem* in the sense that the whites' very lack of awareness of their unwitting pressure upon the Black people is the underlying cause of the problem.

The voices of Yellow Americans have been seldom heard. Therefore the white community tended to assume that the "Orientals" had been well "assimilated" and therefore had no problems. In fact, the white community often used the Yellow Americans as an example the Blacks should emulate and an argument against the Black movement.

The American culture is constructed in such a way that it is considered a right and a responsibility for a person to shout out for his own interest, but it is not considered a responsibility for a person or a community to pay attention to those who are quiet, or to be aware of the possibility that one may be stepping on someone else's toes. American democracy has been based on the philosophy of majority rule, i.e., domination by quantity, or, more precisely, legitimation of a homogenizing domination by the force of large numbers. The inadequacy of this philosophy is becoming increasingly apparent.

This problem, of course, is not limited to the U.S.A. For the Koreans in Japan, for the Gypsies in Sweden, and for many ethnic minorities in other countries the situation is similar or even worse. Many of the members of the dominant culture are unaware of the detrimental effects of their culture upon the ethnic minority groups.

The U.S. has begun to become aware of this problem. I hope that by listening to the voices of the Yellow Americans in addition to those of the Red, Brown and Black Americans, the white community will increase their understanding of the situation and take action to eliminate the white side of the problem by fostering recognition of, respect for, and appreciation of minority cultures among White people. This in turn, I hope, will stimulate an increased awareness of the majority problems in other countries as well.

BORN ITALIAN:
Color Me Red, White, and Green

RUDOLPH J. VECOLI

ETHNICITY, which for some is a recent discovery, has been for me a lifelong preoccupation. The current dialogue over ethnic identity is something I have been carrying on with myself for almost half a century. I have always known that I was born Italian and that this circumstance profoundly affected my life. Even when I pretended to be one of "them" at an Ivy League university or in the Department of State, I knew that beneath my vested grey flannel suit there beat the heart of an Italian boy.

My life has been a journey through cultures and institutions far removed from my immigrant home; mine has been the career of the mobile, rootless academic. Yet through it all, despite university education, travel, and marriage to a non-Italian, and even when I wished otherwise, my ethnic identity has retained a powerful grip on me. My autobiography thus has been a prime source for my exploration of the meaning of ethnicity. If my story were truly singular, there would be little point in discussing it; but this biography is in some ways common to over three million second-generation Italian Americans. This is what makes the experience ethnic and not merely idiosyncratic. I bring to this subject, then, not only the discipline of the historian, but also hopefully the "intelligent subjectivity," to use Michael Novak's term, of an ethnic American.

To be born in America of Italian parents, speak Italian as one's first language, and be raised on *polenta* (not spaghetti,

Mr. Vecoli, Professor of History and Director of the Center for Immigration Studies at the University of Minnesota, Twin Cities, reports that the high point of his career was when he gave a paper in Italian at a conference on Italian emigration in the Sala dei Armi of the Palazzo Vecchio in 1969.

117

since we were *Toscani*) is still not to be an Italian. My first given name was Calvin, after the illustrious president in whose term of office I was born. Thank heaven, it was changed to that of the famous movie star; not because the priest objected, but because my father's friends said that to them Calvin sounded like *cavolo* (cabbage). I was raised in a factory town in Connecticut, and my first memories are of the grim Depression years. My father was a construction laborer and there were long stretches of unemployment. My mother worked in a dress factory, a sweatshop, to eke out the family budget. There were breadlines that my sisters and I stood in to receive rations of flour, milk, and canned beef from Argentina. And yet we never suffered real privation; I don't remember once going to bed hungry. My mother was and is a fabulous cook; I didn't realize until much later that I was eating gourmet meals throughout my childhood. I remember the worry and anxiety as our parents strove mightily to keep us clothed and fed, but they did it. My father came home many nights with his shoulders broken open from carrying the hod. These are memories with which many of my generation of Italian Americans live, but of which we seldom speak. Our immigrant parents were the exploited proletariat of the 1920's and '30's, the factory workers, the miners, the laborers. Not only exploited, but despised to boot as foreigners, as "Dagoes" and "Wops." The insecurity and shame of those years throw a long shadow over the psychic landscape of my generation. No wonder we are anxious to protect our gains, however modest; they are hard won.

My parents, like most Italian immigrants, came from peasant stock. A heritage of centuries of unremitting toil on the land taught them to accept life as it came, a fatalism unrelieved by illusions. Life was a pilgrimage; everyone had a cross to bear. Still, all the more reason to enjoy the good things, especially food and wine, and the companionship of relatives and friends. The children were imbued with the virtues of obedience and respect. If the teacher punished a child for misbehavior, the parent did not protest; rather he administered a second punishment for good measure. Strict discipline, sometimes moderated by affection, was the rule in the Italian American household. No wonder that those of us raised under such a regimen despair at the willfulness of our children. Hard work was the lot of man, at least of the *contadini* if not of the *signori*. We were expected to contribute to the family income as soon as we were of working age. For my sisters this meant leaving school for the factory at fourteen. Being the youngest and coming of age during the war, I was able to continue in high school while working a shift in a factory.

But the "Protestant ethic" and high ambition were not part of our heritage. My father aspired for me to become a barber or shoemaker. After all, he was a laborer all his life; from his point of view, to become an artisan was a significant step upward. More than most other ethnic groups, the Italian Americans have persisted in the ranks of blue-collar workers. It is only in the third and fourth generations that a significant number are entering the professions, the academic careers, the corporate and government bureaucracies. This was due not only to restricted opportunities, though the barriers of prejudice were real enough, but also to the ethnic values which prized family solidarity over individual advancement. Though there were exceptions, education was often viewed as an alien influence which eroded parental control—as in fact it did. Sociological studies suggest that Italians were less characterized by the "achievement syndrome" than were, say, Jews, Greeks, or Japanese. This helps to explain the relatively more limited occupational and spatial mobility of the Italians. The converse of this is the higher degree of stability of the Italian American family and neighborhood.

Formal religion was not an important influence in my youth. Although a devout Catholic, my mother seldom attended church. Like many Italians she found the church of the Irish (there was no Italian priest or parish in our town) alien and cold. A few years ago I visited the church in which my mother worshipped as a girl in a small town in Tuscany. A Romanesque church a thousand years old, it was dark and cool even in mid-July. Banks of votive lamps, the smell of incense, statues of saints and martyrs, the offerings of the faithful for special graces covering the walls—all these had been lacking in America. So she preferred to pray at home. It was the experience of many Italians that the Catholic Church they found in America was strange and sometimes hostile. Like politics, it was dominated by their major antagonists, the Irish. Only in dense settlements where the Italians could have a national parish with Italian priests, venerate the saints of their villages, and celebrate their feast days, were they able to maintain their religious traditions. Although in recent decades many Italian Americans have become more integrated within the Church, religious institutions did not provide the Italians an organizational structure for community life as they did the Poles and Irish.

Like many of the Italian immigrants, my father was a sojourner in this land. He had come with the intention of working for a few years, saving money, and returning to his village. But he remained for a half-century. It was only after he had retired that he returned as an *Americano* to live the last years of his life comfortably on his social security. My father resisted Americanization, although he became a citizen when it was necessary to qualify for the W.P.A. He continued to live like the peasant he was. Rising at daybreak to tend his gardens which produced more vegetables than we could consume, raising rabbits which my mother prepared *alla cacciatora*, making and drinking a hundred gallons of wine a year, setting snares for birds which we ate with *polenta*, playing boccie and cards at the *Società Libero Pensiero* (the Americans did not know it, but this was the Free Thought Society). A man of great physical strength, he worked under driving bosses. He was ill used, and he knew it. One of his favorite expressions, said with bitterness, was, "America biznis" ("America is business").

This too is a memory which lurks in the recesses of the Italian American psyche. This land was not hospitable to the Italians. Our hearts are not full of gratitude, because we know the price that was paid for that which we enjoy today, a price paid in sweat, tears, and blood; the cliché is nonetheless true. How many thousands of Italian immigrants were killed and mutilated in industrial accidents and mine disasters God only knows. They along with the Slavs were the dung, as Louis Adamic put it, which fertilized the growth of America's industrial might. To the wounds of the flesh were added the hurts of the spirit, because they knew only too well that in the view of many Americans they were considered less than dirt. It is not surprising that in moments of despair an imprecation came to their lips: "*Accidenti all' America i a quell Colombo che la scoperta*" ("Curses on America and that Columbus who discovered her"). My father endured; he would not be bent or broken. When I was a child I was ashamed of him because he was not "American." This too we remember, that America has taught children to be ashamed of their parents. As I grew older I came to respect him for his integrity.

I was not raised in a "Little Italy"; thus my experience was significantly different from those who grew up immersed in an Italian American environment. There life was even more ethnically vivid and all-encompassing, because more insulated from American influences. One can still find such enclaves in the North End of Boston, South Brooklyn, the South Side of Philadelphia, the North Ward of Newark, the West Side of Cleveland, the West Side of Chicago, neighborhoods which have proved amazingly resistant to change, to pressures of changing population patterns, and to the designs of city planners. The ethnic character (peasant, if you will) comes through in the fierce attachment to family and neighborhood. Their row houses with madonnas in the small front yards and decal flags in the windows, their grocery stores replete with Italian delicacies, their social clubs, and their churches, these are their social world. To the social planners, attachment to such modest surroundings is incomprehensible. Why don't they join the throngs fleeing to the open spaces of the suburbs? It is not primarily limited means but rather the preference for the dense texture of social relationships of the old neighborhood that holds them despite declining municipal services, rising crime rates, and all the other ills of our sick cities. Of course, many have left; but the Italians, more than any other white ethnic group, appear determined to stay. This also accounts, of course, for the fact that the Italians are locked in conflict with Blacks in many cities. They often are the only whites left.

Ours was a mixed neighborhood. We lived among Germans, Irish, Hungarians, and Poles. I also attended an integrated school, not racially integrated, since there was only one Black family in the town, but including all ethnic and socio-economic groups, from the Yankees who lived in the big houses on the hill to the "Hunkies" and "Dagoes" from the valley. These contacts did not dilute our ethnic consciousness, rather they sharpened it. The pattern of ethnic relationships reflected a hierarchy of groups, with the new immigrants occupying the bottom stratum. As I grew older I became aware of other spheres of American society far removed from the immigrants' world. A prestigious prep school was located in my home town, and Yale University was only a few miles away. These became, in my imagination, symbols of another world, a world of wealth and privilege far beyond the reach of an Italian boy of working-class background. Yet they stimulated my ambition to gain access to that WASP world (as I imagined it) of cultural refinement and cool confidence. More boys from my neighborhood went to reform school than to college, but I early set my sights on higher education as the ladder to that world.

It has been a long journey, psychologically as well as physically. My educational experience was totally alien to my family and ethnic background. In eighteen years of schooling, the only instance in which my Italian origins were recognized as a possible source of pride occurred in kindergarten! Curious how well I remember the teacher commenting to my mother, after I had painted a picture of an ocean liner with red smokestacks, that I might become another Michelangelo. Actually I have never been able to draw, but that comment did wonders for my morale. We now know how important it is that schools give positive reinforcement to a child's self-image. Erik Erikson and others have pointed out the necessity for continuity between self-identity in childhood and adulthood if an individual is to experience wholeness. How deficient our schools have been in this respect, and how deficient they remain. My schooling served to inculcate within me only negative feelings regarding my origins. By omission, and at times explicitly, I was made to feel that there was nothing of value, nothing worthy in my Italianness. Never once, from elementary through graduate school, was the fact that I was fluent in Italian remarked upon as an asset.

This, we know, has been a common experience of immigrant children, as it has been of black, brown, and red children. What a cruel commentary upon the inhumanity and stupidity of the American educational system! No wonder it has failed so many generations of the children of the outsiders, the poor, the alien, the racially and culturally different. But what should one expect? American schools were designed to assimilate, to standardize, to wipe out diversity. Being an obedient, ambitious Italian boy, I tried diligently to assimilate. I embraced the liberal creed of progress and enlightenment; I decried the benighted outlook of working-class ethnics; I sought to model myself after the cosmopolitan, sophisticated intellectual. I succeeded in part, and I did learn a great deal in the process. Yet I could never completely forget who I was. I gradually came to realize that much of what I was trying to be and to believe was at odds with my true self, with my sense of reality, my values, my loyalties. Not only could I never be an authentic WASP; I did not want to be one.

When I went to graduate school, responding to some inner compulsion, I chose to write my dissertation on the Italian immigration, at that time hardly an "in" subject. I have since specialized in immigration and ethnic history. The questions raised by my own autobiography—questions of identity, group life, assimilation, and social policies—have become the issues to which I have sought to address myself in my historical studies. Perhaps it is not surprising that my researches have tended to confirm my autobiographical insights. Another way of putting it would be that by accepting and affirming my own ethnicity I acquired a new perspective on American history, one which liberated me from the conventional interpretations based upon progressive and consensus assumptions. This, of course, is not a unique discovery on my part. Perhaps moved by similar personal as well as scholarly insights, a school of "new pluralists" is emerging to challenge traditional views of American society.

"The Rediscovery of Ethnicity," we must understand, has been a rediscovery on the part of the intellectual community. The ethnic groups, as well as the politicians, priests, and realtors who deal with them, have known about ethnicity all along. What has been termed a resurgence of ethnicity is rather the eruption into public view of passions and attitudes which have long existed submerged in the private worlds of ethnic life.

The ethnics have found their voice; they will be heard. For the first time in their history, the Italian Americans are speaking and being listened to in the militant tones of a Geno Baroni, a Steve Adubato, a Paul Asciolla. But what they are saying must be understood in terms of their history, a history which I have tried to personalize through autobiography. Just as the rhetoric of Black leaders is freighted with a history of long-endured oppression, so the ethnic spokesmen are expressing resentments and frustrations rooted in decades of neglect, abuse, and indignity. There are a hundred such ethnic histories of which we know little or nothing. If we are to understand and to cope with the "new pluralism" it behooves us to study those histories.

ETHNICITY AND THE RECOVERY OF REGIONAL IDENTITY IN APPALACHIA:

Thoughts Upon Entering the Zone of Occult Instability

DAVID E. WHISNANT

> Therapeutic as well as reformist efforts verify the sad truth that in any system based on suppression, exclusion, and exploitation, the oppressed, excluded, and exploited unconsciously accept the evil image they are made to represent by those who are dominant.
>
> Erik Erikson, *Identity: Youth and Crisis*

> The struggle begins with men's recognition that they have been destroyed.
>
> Paolo Freire, *Pedagogy of the Oppressed*

> We will only be heard by American society as we find the means and the courage to speak as a united people.
>
> Warren Wright of Letcher County, Kentucky, December 4, 1971

APPALACHIAN PEOPLE are among the growing number of ethnic and cultural groups which are rejecting the melting pot —together with its associated ideology—and consciously turning to their historical and cultural roots as a source of pride, strength, and political identity. The signs are numerous: Mother Jones posters, with the caption "Pray for the Dead; Fight Like Hell for the Living" pasted in store windows; an Appalachian identity center in Cincinnati's Appalachian ghetto; students deciding to stay and fight for their homes in the mountains, instead of being channeled out by universities controlled by coal and chemical companies.[1] At long last the melting pot

---

Mr. Whisnant, currently on leave from the English Department of the University of Illinois, is working on a book on Appalachian development strategies. He is himself a native of Appalachia.

124

is being viewed as an inadequate and exploitative model of political and social reality—an index to the cultural imperialism that is basic to the American system. If the movement continues the melting pot may in time be replaced by a more sophisticated pluralistic view of culture that is not only more humane in theory but is also more congruent with the rich history and complex present of the Appalachian region.

Where does the movement for a regional consciousness or identity come from? It is obviously not based upon strictly ethnic identification, as is clear by comparing it to movements among Blacks, Chicanos, or Indians. Nor is it an expression of ethnic identity in a looser WASP sense. The WASP image of Appalachia is largely the result of biased historiography. Appalachia is certainly no less WASPish that the rest of the country, but it is nevertheless very mixed ethnically. Communities of Blacks, Indians, Hungarians, Poles, and other ethnic groups dot the mountains. Appropriately enough, the working miners chosen recently by the Miners for Democracy to oppose Tony Boyle in the U.M.W. election are named Arnold Miller, Harry Patrick, and Mike Trbovich.[2] Thus anyone who wishes to understand the current movement toward regional identity must look beyond simple ethnicity, however strictly or loosely defined.

The most important source for the movement may be a shared *sense* of struggle among Appalachian people. There has always been struggle in the mountains, of course, but—except for the union organizing struggles of the twenties and thirties—it has until recently been fragmented, sporadic, and frequently internecine. But now there is a shared perception that Appalachian people are struggling against an attempt by mainstream America and its powerful vested interests to contain, subjugate, and destroy a region, its people, the few remaining fragments of their culture.[3] Whether this perception is accurate is not important here. People are united by the *perception*, nevertheless.

Closely related to the fact of common perception is the political coalition of separate problem- and issue-related struggle groups. Parents on welfare in Appalachia engage in controversy with the school board over the administration of school lunch programs, only to learn that politics dominated by energy conglomerates controls the schools. Having discovered that ubiquitous fact of life in the region, they naturally form alliances with Black Lung, election reform, and anti-stripmining groups. Other coalitions develop as group after group discovers the sordid, interlocking details of the corrupt political, economic, and social system in Appalachia.

From coalition with struggle groups inside the region it is but one step to coalition with groups outside. We have traditionally taken a perverse comfort in believing that Appalachian problems are "special"—aberrations in the system that luckily are not characteristic of all of America. When the President's Appalachian Regional Commission issued its recommendations for the region in 1964, it reported that it had found "a record of insufficiency—a history of traditional acts *not* performed, of American patterns *not* fulfilled."[4] Appalachian people know better. They know that the tragedy at Buffalo Creek, far from being an act of God as the Pittston Coal Company claimed, resulted from private greed, corporate cynicism, and governmental corruption of a perfectly standard American variety.[5] Appalachian people know that historically their problems are in many ways similar to those of Blacks, Indians, Chicanos, migrants, and welfare families in the cities. They are beginning to view the Appalachian Regional Commission as merely a new Bureau of Indian Affairs—a massive, insensitive, imperialistic, paternalistic bureaucracy serving the interests of the rich and the powerful, and extending the hegemony of a culture based on greed, materialism, militarism, and ruinous competition. Thus Appalachian struggle groups increasingly find bonds of common interest with struggle groups elsewhere: to stop the depredation of their lands and people and resources, and to build pride in themselves and their heritage. Recent issues of the weekly *Mountain Eagle* of Whitesburg, Kentucky carried articles about threats of stripmining in Wyoming and Montana by Kennecott Copper, whose subsidiary Peabody Coal has already ruined much of Appalachia.[6] And a recent *Mountain Life and Work* described the plight of Toledo City in the Philippines, site of the largest copper mine in Asia. "Toledo," said the writer, "is a classic mining town . . . [whose] problems are not unlike the ones faced by . . . mining towns in West Virginia."

Another source for the movement is radical politics. Let me not overgeneralize here, for I do not believe armed revolution is imminent in the mountains—although if it came it wouldn't be the first time; the history of the mountains is far more radical, after all, than Jack Weller knew. Nevertheless, mountain people are being radicalized—partly by reading radical political analyses of their problems, and partly through the efforts of a few radical organizers, but mostly through the natural process of looking about them at the state of their own social and political system. One mountaineer said recently it took him fifty years to be radicalized, but that the strippers are now radicalizing kids of twelve and thirteen. Letcher County's Warren Wright, whose eighteen-month losing battle to keep Bethlehem Steel from stripping his land is known throughout the mountains, said his struggle made him "socially alive for the first time."

Less important than—but related to—radical politics as a source is what has been called the counter-culture. I do not expect to see geodesic domes made from the tops of abandoned automobiles sprouting all over the mountains any time soon (although abandoned automobiles are certainly plentiful enough), or to hear the Hare Krishna chanted from every mountain top, but I do expect a strengthening and elaboration of the perception that some aspects of traditional Appalachian culture are remarkably similar to the counter-culture—its personalism, informal life styles, relationship to the land and to specific places, its essentially sacred reading of human experience, and so on.

But how is the movement expressing itself? What forms is it taking? I have already mentioned that one source of Appalachian identity is working alliances among struggle groups. The reverse is also true: as the movement gains momentum, more working alliances are formed. The sixty-year-old Council of the Southern Mountains, until several years ago a relatively conservative organization, now works with the activist East Kentucky Welfare Rights Organization, the People's Appalachian Research Collective, Save Our Kentucky, Mountain People's Rights, Federation of Communities in Service, and other groups. Transcending inevitable differences in policy and philosophy is a sense of common purpose with others in the struggle.

The movement is also expressing itself in efforts to reform and gain control of the region's institutions—especially its educational system. James Branscome has said that Appalachian schools are "daylight detention camps" which insist that "all of us become nice melting-pot products who behave like Dick and Jane." While it is conventional to say that the schools have "failed" in Appalachia, Branscome charges that they have "succeeded marvelously in doing what [they were] designed to do: obliterate differences and adjust children to the technological society as unquestioning, joyless, and obedient robots."[7] At the very least, schools in Appalachia can be charged with a massive dereliction of responsibility. They have served the vested economic and political interests of the region well; they have served its people almost not at all. Most Appalachian universities address themselves to a national constituency as they strive, like so many Mark the Match Boys, to make it—and the region itself be damned.

But change is in the air. A March, 1972 regional self-government conference at Virginia Polytechnic Institute focused partly on V.P.I. itself—the composition of its governing board, its allocation of resources, its potential for service in the region. Conference participants charged that V.P.I. was serving the interests of the coal and chemical companies and urged that an Appalachian People's Board of Visitors be established to monitor the institution.*

Parents of secondary school children who five years ago felt guilty because their children couldn't make it on the Dick and Jane scale are questioning the scale itself, asking who controls the schools, and for whose benefit. In the process they are beginning to define an Appalachian education system that serves their legitimate interests and fosters pride in their identity. As two young Appalachian workers wrote recently in *Mountain Life and Work:* "It is time to foster a new education in our midst. . . . Education in Appalachia is so bad because it tries to do what education outside Appalachia tries to do. Only

---

*An example of the legitimacy of the radicals' claim that V.P.I., a state-supported institution, is a captive of the coal industry may be found in Tom Bethell's *The Hurricane Creek Massacre* (New York, 1972), a study of the Leslie County, Kentucky mine disaster that killed thirty-eight men in December, 1970. Bethell shows that the Nixon administration attempted to sabotage the Federal Coal Mine Health and Safety Act of 1969 by removing all Bureau of Mines personnel who were inclined to enforce its provisions, including Bureau Director John O'Leary. After leaving the Bureau without a director for two months, Nixon nominated J. Richard Lucas, director of mineral engineering at V.P.I., who held a $200,000 investment portfolio of mining stocks, earned high fees as a coal industry consultant, and had "apparently plagiarized part of his doctoral thesis."

if we cut ourselves away from the dominant standards of productivity and prosperity can we begin to bring ourselves together in the mountains."[8]

The media are also being criticized for aiding the exploitation of Appalachian people, and now they are being pressured by groups interested in defining a regional identity. Networks which have long since discontinued "Amos 'n' Andy" and other racist programs and which have shown some signs recently of reassessing their sexist images of women, continue to run such shows as "Hee Haw" and "Green Acres" and "The Beverly Hillbillies." Al Capp's "Li'l Abner" appears in virtually every hometown newspaper. In their gross insensitivity to the feelings of Appalachian people, to their spiritual and material needs, and to the richness and vitality of their culture, the media have been agents of a broader pattern of cultural imperialism.[9]

But some of those supposedly fatalistic, tradition-bound hillbillies Jack Weller wrote about in his condescending *Yesterday's People*[10] are challenging the media these days. In some cases they are forming their own alternative media, such as the Appalachian Film Workshop in Whitesburg, Kentucky, which has produced—using local skills only—films on Appalachian people, history, culture, and struggle. Underground newspapers are to be found here and there—at least until, like the very effective *Hawkeye*, they are burned out by those whose privileges they expose and threaten. There are also signs that mountain people will be challenging the licenses of established radio and television stations under the new FCC ruling on local programming. In response to that ruling, one large West Virginia station filled its prime-time, local programming slot with "Wagon Train"—five nights a week. In at least one Appalachian community, a young Nader-type lawyer has begun working to challenge such cynical practices. Disgusted with official inaction on stripmining in the mountains, and convinced that "the channels . . . will not speak for us, do not hear us, and have in simple truth betrayed us," two hundred mountain people assembled in December, 1971 for a People's Hearing on Strip Mining. Speaker Warren Wright explicitly condemned the media, and insisted that ways be found to bypass them.*

*Thus far, however, no Appalachian struggle group has formed its own radio or television station, as have one or two American Indian groups. On the People's Hearing, see *MLW*, XLVII (November, 1971), 22ff.

A final comment upon the forms the struggle for regional identity is taking before passing to the question of the worth and durability of the movement. Movements of this type usually find expression in a new iconography and in the generation of cultural heroes around whom identity and solidarity can form. Who those heroes will be in the mountains is not yet clear. But it won't be Li'l Abner or the Federal Cochairman of the Appalachian Regional Commission. Nor will it be Che Guevara, for radicals in the mountains know there is no need to import heroes; Appalachian history is full of them. But it may be the legendary Mother Jones, who suffered and fought through so many of the mining struggles in the mountains. Or the Widow Combs, who in 1965, at the age of sixty-one, sat down in front of bulldozers to keep her land from being stripped. "We live hard," she told the deputies who came to carry her to jail. "This land and this house is all we've got. Go on and leave us alone."*

But how durable and useful will all of this be? What actual effects has it had and will it continue to have in the region? At the very least, the movement has great psychological value. As Paolo Freire, Frantz Fanon and others have pointed out, oppressed people need solidarity and a sense of shared identity for their own psychological reasons, regardless of whether they are or soon will be in a position to control their political and social destiny.[11] The paradox of the Appalachian situation—indeed of all such situations—is that the oppressors *deny* the identity oppressed people wish for themselves at the same time that they *supply* an undesirable identity—one which is psychologically destructive, socially demeaning, and calculated to serve the manipulative interests of the oppressor.

The movement also has a "monkey wrench" function. It presents an open challenge to conventional wisdom, not only to its operative images, metaphors, and models but also to the policies and programs that result. Those among whom the sense of Appalachian identity and solidarity is strongest are also those most likely to view the War on Poverty as a fiasco and the Appalachian Regional Commission as a new Bureau of Indian

*On the Widow Combs, Dan Gibson, and Jink Ray, all of whose heroism in the Appalachian struggle is frequently celebrated at Appalachian gatherings, see *Appalachian People's History Book* (Louisville: Southern Conference Educational Fund, 1970), pp. 97ff.

Affairs. Nor is it accidental that citizens of Letcher County, Kentucky recently forced the County Planning Commission to abandon a plan that would benefit developers and highway builders while displacing local people from their homes and destroying their way of life.[12]

Besides challenging conventional wisdom on a day-to-day basis, the movement is also forcing the writing of a revisionist history of the region. Only ignorance of the generations of struggle and heroism in the mountains allows anyone to speak glibly of the "fatalism" and "traditionalism" of Appalachian people. The perceptive anthropologist Helen Lewis has recently suggested that what has perennially been called fatalism in Appalachian character may in fact have been simple powerlessness in the face of an overwhelmingly powerful coal industry.[13] But revisionist history is far from official recognition or acceptance, and thus it remains to organizations like the Southern Conference Education Fund to issue an *Appalachian People's History Book* designed to teach children about the Wataugans, anti-slavery movements in the mountains, Black Appalachians, the Coal Creek War and the convict lease system, Paint Creek and Cabin Creek, the Battle of Evarts and the death of Harry Simms, and so on down to the real story of Buffalo Creek in this year of grace 1973.[14]

And finally, it is inevitable that a revisionist view of the problems of a major region of the United States should ultimately force a revisionist view of aspects of American experience generally. The movement for Appalachian identity has as one of its major by-products the strong suggestion that the mainstream is polluted, if I may borrow an ecological metaphor. Many young people—and not a few older people—simply no longer agree with the President's Appalachian Regional Commission that the region's problems result from "a history . . . of American patterns *not* fulfilled." On the contrary, they believe that American patterns *have* been fulfilled with a vengeance in Appalachia—patterns of greed, of political corruption, of laws and tax structures favoring the rich, of callous disregard for the environment—and that that fact has spelled Appalachia's doom. Thus when Alvin Arnett, Executive Director of the Appalachian Regional Commission, declares that certain areas of Appalachia might reasonably be depopulated and turned over entirely to the coal companies, his statement is viewed inside the region not as the mumblings of a madman but as a coldly logical extension of certain core assumptions, structures, and values in American life.[15] The inescapable conclusion is endlessly recited by activists in the region: Appalachia's future will be bright in proportion to people's ability to find solutions *outside* the norms and assumptions of the American system.

By outside the system I do not necessarily mean revolutionary in any narrow political sense. I mean simply that some people in the region are talking seriously of using public wealth—especially mineral resources and hydroelectric power—for the public good as they have rarely been used in America; of building an educational system that respects individual differences and the few precious cultural distinctions that remain among us despite our determined efforts to eradicate them; of developing a social system based on a reasonable level of resource use and decent concern for unborn generations; of moving beyond simplistic free enterprise models of the social order to a complex understanding of what really produces the sick and the poor, the alienated and the unemployed, the haves and the have nots in our society.

Thus the stirrings I have described are quite understandably viewed in some quarters as a threat to the present order. And they are being opposed, not usually by overt force or violence (though both have been used upon occasion), but by those forms of pressure the system is so marvelously articulated to supply: the denial of funds, the buying of candidates and elections, the transferring and firing of personnel, the selective enforcement of laws and regulations.

But so far this has been an "external" statement on the movement—written as if the problem were merely to describe what is going on "out there" in Appalachia. Actually I am capable of no such detachment or objectivity. I was born and raised in the Appalachian mountains, and as Utah Phillips' song "The Green Rolling Hills of West Virginia" says, "They keep me and never let me go." Hence the movement I have described is actually occurring both in the Appalachia that is in my head and in the one that is "out there." The truth is that I *cannot* separate them; to do so I would have to have had a different past. The problem of description is inseparable from the problem of *relation*. To admit this is inevitably to add a personal and even spiritual dimension to the historical and political phenomenon I have described.

I lived in the mountains until I was about eighteen—not in a coal camp or a remote holler, but in a village maintained by one of the first large chemical industries to bring "progress" to the region. One of my earliest memories is of seeing a once clear stream near my home run sluggishly with its burden of chemical waste. Another is of smelling carbon disulfide in the air twenty-four hours a day. I would like to be able to say that those sights and smells made me determined at the tender age of twelve to fight the forces that were destroying the homeland I loved and was determined to live in all my days. But that isn't the case. As Branscome has said, the system does its work well. The institutions which influenced my life—the church, the public schools, the media—had the cumulative effect of impelling me out of Appalachia, both physically and psychologically.

At the age of eighteen I left the mountains for Georgia Tech. True to my Dick and Jane conditioning, I worked diligently and did well. Ultimately I would have taken a job with North American or Dow or Standard Oil but for one fact: I began rather randomly to read some books from a list handed to me at the end of a term by an English professor: James, *The Varieties of Religious Experience*; de Tocqueville, *Democracy in America*; Eugene O'Neill; Sinclair Lewis; W. J. Cash, *The Mind of the South*; Thomas Wolfe; Henry Adams; Alfred North Whitehead; Dreiser; David Reisman. That reading, I now recognize, called everything into question. It provided not only the rudiments of an analysis of the American system counter to that which I had accepted from the institutions and authorities I knew, but also the germ of an impulse that fifteen years later would take me back to Appalachia.

One way of measuring my life between my twenty-first and thirty-fourth years would be to apply the conventional yardstick of my success in accomplishing what the system trained me to accomplish: a doctorate, a teaching job at a major university, publications, recognition as a scholar and teacher. But it could also be measured as a series of attempts to resolve a deep tension between trying to do what I had been taught to do and told was worth doing, and trying to find what my compatriot Thomas Wolfe would have called my lost self—the authentic self that was struggling to be born out of my own resources and those of my homeland. And not only to be born, but to find work worth doing. An unsympathetic critic might charge that I was merely the victim of a perpetual adolescent identity crisis. An alternative explanation that is at least possible is that I was (and am) trying to resolve a dilemma that has its basis in the very structure of American life.

Our culture demands and rewards atomistic, mobile individuals. Attachment to place, or kin, or particular cultural contexts is branded nostalgic or impractical, both of which are implicitly antisocial. Hence an attempt to relate to one's origins involves one not only in the tactical problem of sorting out his own personal history, but also in the strategic problem of threading his way tortuously through the maze of laws, conventions, structures, and institutions that impel him to do otherwise.

What guideposts or principles have I found that point the way through that maze? Unfortunately, very few. Except for scattered remarks by Edgar Friedenberg, Robert Coles, and a few others, I have found only two essays that speak pointedly to the problem: Frantz Fanon's "The Pitfalls of National Consciousness" and "On National Culture" in *The Wretched of the Earth*.[16] Now Appalachia is not Algeria, I readily admit, but I share the judgment of many that Appalachia may legitimately be viewed as a colony.[17] In any event, I see myself repeatedly in Fanon's analysis of the situation of native intellectuals in a colony going through decolonization.

Like many radicals, Fanon understood the function of careerism in maintaining any form of economic and political domination: it gives the individual a stake in the assumptions, dynamics, and (particularly) the reward structure of the system. Long before I read Fanon, however, I had reached essentially this conclusion myself—though I conceived and expressed it in less consciously political terms—and had rejected the careerist model for my own personal development.[18] Reading Fanon simply focused the issue sharply in the context of my returning to Appalachia: I cannot do it in terms of any even remotely conventional careerist aims. This is true not only because the training I was given by the system fitted me more to *leave* than stay and help, but also because the value of any person in the Appalachian struggle that lies ahead will be in direct proportion to his ability to put the struggle itself above careerist aims.

And this is more than piety, it seems to me; it is an elemental political and economic fact which derives from the system's characteristic unwillingness to reward its critics.

Fanon asserts, after all, that "In an underdeveloped country an authentic national middle class . . . [must] betray the calling fate has màrked out for it, and put at the people's disposal the intellectual and technical capital that it has snatched when going through the colonial universities."[19] I am acutely aware, then, that I am a beneficiary of precisely that system which has colonized and destroyed Appalachia. I cannot erase my history, but perhaps I can use my skills in a way that the system never intended, and help reverse to some degree the collusion of intellectuals and the power elite that has brought so much grief to Appalachia—as indeed it has to the rest of the country. I have no doubt that the wisdom of the Appalachian Regional Commission's depopulation strategy will be elegantly supported by some academic economists and sociologists *inside* Appalachia. Their proposals will get them grants, and their articles will earn them promotions.

Thus one implication of rejecting careerism in returning to Appalachia is that I cannot *serve the same interests*. But there is another: I must not conceive of myself as an expert who always knows what is good for people. From that attitude derive counterproductive style and tactics. If care is taken, says Fanon, "to use only a language that is understood by graduates in law and economics, you can easily prove that the masses have to be managed from above. But . . . if you are not obsessed by the perverse desire to spread confusion and rid yourself of the people, then you will realize that the masses are quick to seize every shade of meaning and to learn all the tricks of the trade . . . . The business of obscuring language is a mask behind which stands out the much greater business of plunder. The people's property and the people's sovereignty are to be stripped from them at one and the same time. Everything can be explained to the people, on the single condition that you really want them to understand."[20]

Put another way, Fanon's point is that those who choose to change their allegiance from the powerful to the powerless do not thereby necessarily escape the tendency (no less frequent among intellectuals and professionals than among people generally) to act primarily out of their own deep yearning for self-esteem. But Paolo Freire says that "Those who authentically commit themselves to the people must re-examine themselves constantly. This conversion is so radical as not to allow ambiguous behavior."[21] And yet for me the situation is fraught with unavoidable ambiguities and ambivalences that must somehow be sorted out. To remain nostalgically attached to my *immediate* past—in which I filled (albeit uncomfortably and reluctantly) the role of expert in the exploitative system—is to deny a regenerative impulse and thus to foreclose the possibility of usefulness in the struggle. Yet to be uncritically sensitive to the regenerative impulse—based as it undeniably is to some degree in nostalgia for my *Appalachian* past—is to blind myself to the real nature of the *present* struggle.

Fanon resolves the problem of the possibly regressive nature of the recovery of national (or regional or personal) identity by insisting that one go back not to what was (or maybe never was), but to what *is* and what is emerging, and by insisting that one must go not merely to observe and feel, but to participate. Speaking of the role of native writers in decolonization movements, he says, "The colonized man who writes for his people ought to use the past with the intention of opening the future, as an invitation to action and a basis for hope. But to ensure that hope and give it form, he must take part in action and throw himself body and soul into the national struggle. You may speak about everything under the sun; but when you decide to speak of that unique thing in a man's life that is represented by the fact of opening up new horizons . . . and by raising yourself and your people to their feet, then you must collaborate on the physical plane." It is not enough, he says, "to try to get back to the people in the past out of which they have already emerged; rather we must join them in that fluctuating movement which they are just giving a shape to, and which, as soon as it has started, will be the signal for everything to be called into question. Let there be no mistake about it; it is to this *zone of occult instability where the people dwell* that we must come; and it is there that our souls are crystallized and that our perceptions and our lives are transfused with light."[22]

I hazard no predictions about how the scales ultimately will tip either for the region or for its hundreds of thousands of hillborn children—now scattered to the far corners of the continent—trying to find themselves and each other. Appalachia in twenty-five years may be Middle America with a vengeance; it may look like that Dantean (indeed that 100% American) landscape between Newark Airport and Manhattan. The Appalachian Regional Commission may have succeeded in pacifying the region by moving everyone but the coal companies out. The only answer for outmigrants may be unwilling adjustment to the demands of an urban-industrial megastate, and to its implications for human personality. Thoreau said that the California gold rush of 1849 revealed with utter clarity what American character really was. That may or may not be true, but the one-hundred-year "rape of the Appalachians," as Harry Caudill has called it, appears to confirm his observation.

During the early years of the century, Appalachian people were congratulated again and again for being "100% pure Anglo-Saxon stock"—loyal Americans to the core. The truth is, however, that Appalachian people have always had an *ambivalent* relationship to the American system. Those supposedly loyal Americans have tangled more times with the Establishment in its various guises than all the New Left put together. So it is likely to be a long and confusing struggle at every level—personal, regional, national. Opposition is formidable, inertia is great, ambivalence is deep. But if there is hope in the present movement, it lies in its attempt to resolve the ambivalence and to assess for the first time the real cost of loyalty.

NOTES

1. See the New York *Times*, "Ideal of Unity Stirs Appalachian Poor," April 23, 1972, p. 1; *People's Appalachia*, I (Oct.-Dec., 1970); and a special education issue of *Mountain Life and Work*, XLVIII (January, 1972). Hereafter cited as *MLW*. An early notice of the movement is Si Kahn's article in *MLW*, XLVI (September, 1970), 10ff.
2. See *MLW*, XLVIII (May, 1972), 3-6. For an excellent study of a Black community in Kentucky, see W. L. Montell, *The Saga of Coe Ridge* (Knoxville: University of Tennessee Press, 1970).
3. See, for example, *MLW*, XLVIII (March, 1972), and *People's Appalachia*, I (June-July, 1970) and I (August-September, 1970).
4. *Appalachia: a Report by the President's Appalachian Regional Commission* (Washington, D.C.: Government Printing Office, 1964), p. 16.
5. See *MLW*, XLVIII (March, 1972), 3-8.
6. *Mountain Eagle*, June 22, 1972, p. 3.

7. James Branscome, "Educating the Disadvantaged: a New Description of the American Dilemma," an address to the Virginia Council on Social Welfare Conference, November 12, 1970 (mimeographed); and "Educating Appalachia's Poor," in *Appalachia's People, Problems, Alternatives: an Introductory Social Science Reader* (Morgantown: People's Appalachian Research Collective, [1971]), pp. 172-175.

8. *MLW*, XLVIII (January, 1972), p. 9.

9. See Branscome, "Educating Appalachia's Poor," in *Appalachia's People, Problems, Alternatives*, p. 172. Also Don West's article in *MLW*, XX (Spring, 1940), 40, perhaps the earliest item on Li'l Abner as an index of cultural imperialism. The fullest statement I have seen is Paul Kaufman's "Who's Afraid of Al Capp?"—an address at West Virginia University, April 16, 1967 (mimeo).

10. Jack Weller, *Yesterday's People: Life in Contemporary Appalachia* (Lexington, Ky., 1965).

11. Paolo Freire, *Pedogogy of the Oppressed* (New York, 1972), and Frantz Fanon, *The Wretched of the Earth* (1963; reprinted New York: Grove Press, 1968).

12. On the A.R.C.-B.I.A. parrallel, see Robb Burlage, "Toward a People's ARC," in David S. Walls, ed., *Appalachia in the Sixties: Decade of Awakening* (Lexington, Ky. 1972), pp. 246-258; and *Appalachia's People, Problems, Alternatives: an Introductory Social Science Reader* (Revised ed., Morgantown: People's Appalachian Research Collective, 1972), p. 276. On the Letcher County planning dispute, see the *Mountain Eagle*, July 27, 1972, p. 1, and subsequent issues.

13. Helen Lewis, "Fatalism or the Coal Industry?," *Mountain Life and Work*, XLVI (December, 1970), 4-15. See also Freire, *Pedagogy of the Oppressed*, p. 48.

14. *Appalachian People's History Book* (Louisville, Ky.: Southern Conference Education Fund, 1970). Some of these incidents are beginning to be treated elsewhere as well. See, for example, Archie Green's excellent chapter on the Coal Creek War in *Only a Miner: Studies in Recorded Coal-Mining Songs* (Urbana, Ill., 1972).

15. Phil Primack, "Depopulation Plan Advanced by ARC Director," Whitesburg (Ky.) *Mountain Eagle*, June 29, 1972, p. 1. Harry Caudill noted the A.R.C's tendencies in this direction in his address "Education for a New Appalachia," April 20, 1967 (mimeo).

16. Fanon, *The Wretched of the Earth*, pp. 148-248.

17. See *People's Appalachia*, I (August-September, 1970).

18. David E. Whisnant, "Career and Calling: A Personal Record and a Tentative Suggestion," *Soundings*, LIII (Summer, 1970), 111-123.

19. Fanon, p. 150. In 1966, Robert F. Munn noted that a 150-page index of all academic historical journals published in West Virginia contained not a single reference to John L. Lewis, the U.M.W., or strikes in the coalfields [*MLW*, XLII (Summer, 1966), 14].

20. Fanon, pp. 188f. Cf. Freire, *Pedagogy of the Oppressed*, pp. 75ff.

21. Freire, p. 47.

22. Fanon, p. 227. (italics added).

A Word about *Soundings*

Since it began publication in 1968 *Soundings* has attracted a growing readership through its unique combination of scholarly competence and boldness. The list of authors published covers a wide spectrum of disciplines and levels of experiences; it is not unusual for an issue to combine contributions from both established scholars and younger members of the academic community. In an era in which there is renewed concern for interdisciplinary discussions bridging the gaps between the natural sciences, the social sciences, and the humanities, *Soundings* has steadily promoted exchanges at a high level of competence and penetration.

Soundings publishes a special issue every year. Its regular issues have included articles by such authors as Michael Polanyi, Rosemary Ruether, Robert Bellah, and Michael Novak and articles on the economics and ethics of pollution control, pop architecture, sexual politics, Latin American political development, and the morality of new medical techniques.

The subscription rates for the journal provide a bargain for hard-pressed scholars interested in interdisciplinary study. At $9 for one year, $15 for two, and $20 for three with student subscriptions at the reduced rate of $6, *Soundings* provides relevant and exciting input four times a year for the concerned reader. *Soundings'* address is P.O. Box 6309, Station B, Nashville, Tennessee 37235.